VANITY FAIR

Vanity Fair is a very vain, wicked, foolish place, full of all sorts of falseness and pretence. It is a place where you gamble and get into debt, and wait for your rich aunt to die. A place where you swear undying love to your sweetheart, and write a love letter to someone else the next day. It is a place where cunning and lies bring rewards. It is a place where men go to war, and women fall in love, a place of laughter, tears, danger, and excitement . . . It is 1815 in London and Brighton, Brussels and Paris.

Becky Sharp and Amelia Sedley are starting out on the great adventure of Vanity Fair. Each will find a husband, but how long will it last? Who will wear diamonds, who will go hungry? Will they be faithful, foolish, neglected, devoted? Who will sew banknotes into her dress and follow a victorious army to Paris? Who will go home to her mother and weep in misery? And their friends and relations . . . Will Joseph Sedley be a fool all his life? Will Rawdon Crawley learn the truth? Will William Dobbin get his heart's desire?

'Oh, the vanity and folly of human wishes! Which of us is happy in this world? Which of us has our heart's desire? Or, having it, is satisfied?'

T0344579

OXFORD BOOKWORMS LIBRARY

Classics

Vanity Fair

Stage 6 (2500 headwords)

Series Editor: Jennifer Bassett
Founder Editor: Tricia Hedge
Activities Editors: Jennifer Bassett and Christine Lindop

WILLIAM MAKEPEACE THACKERAY

Vanity Fair

Retold by
Diane Mowat

Illustrations by William Thackeray
from the engravings in the 1847 edition

OXFORD UNIVERSITY PRESS

OXFORD
UNIVERSITY PRESS

Great Clarendon Street, Oxford, OX2 6DP, United Kingdom

Oxford University Press is a department of the University of Oxford.
It furthers the University's objective of excellence in research, scholarship,
and education by publishing worldwide. Oxford is a registered trade
mark of Oxford University Press in the UK and in certain other countries

This simplified edition © Oxford University Press 2008

The moral rights of the author have been asserted

First published in Oxford Bookworms 2004

24

No unauthorized photocopying

All rights reserved. No part of this publication may be reproduced,
stored in a retrieval system, or transmitted, in any form or by any means,
without the prior permission in writing of Oxford University Press, or as
expressly permitted by law, by licence or under terms agreed with the
appropriate reprographics rights organization. Enquiries concerning
reproduction outside the scope of the above should be sent to the ELT
Rights Department, Oxford University Press, at the address above

You must not circulate this work in any other form and you must
impose this same condition on any acquirer

Links to third party websites are provided by Oxford in good faith and
for information only. Oxford disclaims any responsibility for the materials
contained in any third party website referenced in this work

ISBN: 978 0 19 479269 1   Book
ISBN: 978 0 19 462127 4   Book and audio pack

Printed in China

Word count (main text): 32,940 words

For more information on the Oxford Bookworms Library,
visit www.oup.com/elt/gradedreaders

ACKNOWLEDGEMENTS

Text adapted by Diane Mowat

The illustrations on pages 9, 14, 23, 33, 41, 52, 60, 67, 76, 84, 94,
103, 118 are by kind permission of the Bodleian Library, Oxford.

All illustrations are by William Makepeace Thackeray and are
from the engravings in the 1847 edition of *Vanity Fair*.

Cover image by Getty Images (Henry Clarke/Conde Nast Collection)

CONTENTS

PEOPLE IN THIS STORY

Miss Rebecca (Becky) Sharp

Miss Amelia (Emmy) Sedley
Mr Joseph (Jos) Sedley, *Amelia's brother*
Mr John Sedley, *father of Amelia and Joseph*
Mrs Sedley, *his wife*

Mr George Osborne, *a lieutenant in the army; later, a captain*
Georgy, *George's son*
Mr John Osborne, *father of George Osborne, and grandfather of Georgy*
Miss Jane Osborne } *George's sisters, and Georgy's aunts*
Miss Maria Osborne

Mr William Dobbin, *a captain in the army; later, a major*
Miss Dobbin, *William's sister*

Sir Pitt Crawley, *a baronet*
Mr Pitt (later, Sir Pitt) Crawley, *Sir Pitt's older son (by his first wife)*
Lady Jane Crawley, *Pitt Crawley's wife*
Mr Rawdon Crawley, *Sir Pitt's younger son (by his first wife), a captain in the army; later, a colonel*
Young Rawdon (Rawdy), *Rawdon's son*
Lady Crawley, *Sir Pitt's second wife, mother of Rose and Violet*
Miss Matilda Crawley, *Sir Pitt's unmarried sister, and Rawdon's aunt*
Miss Briggs, *paid companion to Miss Crawley*
Mr Bute Crawley, *Sir Pitt's brother*
Mrs Bute Crawley, *Mr Bute's wife*

Lord Steyne, *a nobleman*

The young ladies leave school

One sunny morning in June, early in the 1800s, Miss Amelia Sedley and Miss Rebecca Sharp left school. The carriage which took them away from Miss Pinkerton's school for young ladies was filled with gifts and flowers for Amelia, for everyone loved her; but nobody cried when Rebecca left.

We are going to see a great deal of Amelia, so there is no harm in saying straight away that she was a dear little creature. She is not a heroine because her nose was rather short and her face was too round, though it shone with rosy health. She had a lovely smile and her eyes were bright with good humour, except when they were filled with tears, which happened a great deal too often because she had the kindest heart in the world. And when she left school she did not know whether to cry or not. She was glad to go home, but she was very sad to leave her friends at school.

Well, at last the goodbyes were over and the carriage drove away. In her hand Amelia held a letter from Miss Pinkerton, the school's headmistress, which was full of praise for Amelia's educational achievements and the sweetness of her nature.

Amelia's companion, Miss Rebecca Sharp, had no letter from Miss Pinkerton, and was not at all sad to leave school. Indeed, she was delighted.

'I hate the place,' she said. 'I never want to see it again! I wish it were at the bottom of the river, with Miss Pinkerton too.'

Amelia was shocked. 'Oh, Rebecca!' she cried. 'How can you have such wicked thoughts?'

As you will guess, Rebecca was not a kind or forgiving person. She said that the world treated her very badly – though it was quite possible that she deserved the treatment she got.

Her father was an artist, who had given drawing lessons to the young ladies at Miss Pinkerton's school. He was a clever man and a pleasant companion, but was always in debt and had too great a fondness for the bottle. When he was drunk, he used to beat his wife and daughter. He had married a French dancer, who had taught her daughter to speak perfect French. She had died young, leaving Rebecca to her father's care.

And when Rebecca was seventeen, her father died. On his deathbed he wrote to Miss Pinkerton, begging her to look after his orphan daughter. So Miss Pinkerton employed Rebecca to speak French to the young ladies. In return, Rebecca lived in the school, was paid a few pounds a year, and was allowed to attend classes when she was free.

Rebecca, or Becky, as she was often called, was small and thin, with a pale face and light red hair. She usually kept her head down, but when she looked up, her green eyes were large and attractive, especially to men. Next to the tall, healthy young ladies in the school, Becky Sharp looked like a child. But being poor and in debt had taught her many adult lessons. She knew how to deal with angry shopkeepers demanding their money, and how to charm them into providing one more meal. Her father, who was very proud of her lively mind, had liked to have her at his drinking parties, though the conversation of his wild friends was hardly suitable for a young girl. But she had never been a girl, she said; she had been a woman since she was eight years old.

Rebecca hated the school. She argued and fought with Miss Pinkerton, and was jealous of the young ladies there. After the freedom of her father's house, the school felt like a prison, and she was soon making plans for her escape.

Her only friend was Amelia Sedley, and when Amelia left school at the age of seventeen, Rebecca, now aged nineteen, left school too. She had obtained a post as a governess to the daughters of Sir Pitt Crawley, to whose house she would go after spending a few weeks with Miss Sedley's family.

By the time the carriage arrived at the Sedleys' house in Russell Square, Amelia had forgotten her sadness and was happy to be home again. She took great pleasure in showing Rebecca every room in the house, her piano, all her books, her dresses, her jewellery, and the wonderful presents which her brother Joseph had brought back for her from India.

'It must be delightful to have a brother,' said Rebecca. 'He's very rich, I expect, if he's been in India. Is his wife very pretty?'

'Oh yes, Joseph is wealthy, but he isn't married,' Amelia said.

'Oh, what a pity!' said Rebecca. 'I was sure you said he was married, and I was hoping to meet your nieces and nephews.'

But the thought that was really going through Rebecca's mind was this: 'If Mr Joseph Sedley is rich and unmarried, why shouldn't I marry him? I have only a few weeks, to be sure, but there's no harm in trying.'

Should we blame Miss Sharp for her marriage ambitions? No, for we must remember that poor Rebecca had no kind mother to arrange this delicate business for her, and that if she did not get a husband for herself, there was no one else to do it for her.

So Rebecca became even more affectionate to Amelia, thanking her with tears in her eyes for the presents which her dear friend had given her. And when the dinner-bell rang, she went downstairs with her arm round her friend's waist, as is the habit of young ladies who love each other dearly.

In the drawing-room they found a large, fat man, fashionably dressed in bright colours, sitting by the fire reading the newspaper. As the young ladies entered, he stood up quickly, and his face went red in alarm and embarrassment.

'It's only your sister, Joseph,' said Amelia, laughing. 'I've finished school, you know, and this is my friend, Miss Sharp. You've heard me talk about her.'

'No, never,' said Joseph in great confusion. 'That is, yes – what very cold weather we're having, Miss—', and he began to stir up the fire, although it was the middle of June.

'He's very handsome,' Rebecca whispered, rather loudly.

'Oh, do you think so?' said Amelia. 'I'll tell him.'

'No, please don't!' cried Miss Sharp, stepping back and keeping her eyes fixed modestly on the carpet.

Joseph Sedley was twelve years older than his sister, and worked in Bengal, in a very isolated place, for the East India Company. But he became ill, and was sent back to London, where he decided to enjoy all the pleasures he had missed when he went to India. So he had his own apartment, drove his horses in the park, ate in fashionable restaurants, and went to the theatre. But he had no friends. He was fat, lazy, and vain, and the sight of a lady frightened him tremendously.

Becky Sharp would have to be very clever indeed to catch such a man for a husband. Her first moves, though, showed considerable skill. 'I must be very quiet,' she thought, 'and very interested in India.' And all through dinner, she paid great attention to everything Joseph said.

After dinner, when the ladies had gone up to the drawing-room, old Mr Sedley laughed, and said to his son, 'Take care, Jos. That girl is planning to catch you for a husband.'

'Nonsense!' Joseph replied. But he could not help thinking about her and the way she had looked at him with her beautiful green eyes when he had picked up her handkerchief. 'She dropped it twice,' he thought. 'And is that her singing now in the drawing-room? Shall I go up and see?'

But his shyness overcame him, and he quietly slipped away from the house. From the window Mrs Sedley saw him go. 'Miss Sharp has frightened him away,' she remarked.

It was three days before Joseph returned to the house, and during that time Rebecca never mentioned his name. She was full of grateful respect for Mrs Sedley, laughed at all Mr Sedley's jokes, and was delighted with every excursion. When Amelia had a headache, Rebecca would not go out without her. Her green eyes filled with tears. 'Dear, dear Emmy,' she said. 'How could I go out and leave you? You have shown a poor orphan what happiness and love are for the first time in her life.'

In fact, Becky Sharp won the hearts of all the family.

On the day that Joseph reappeared, Amelia reminded her brother that he had promised to take her to the Royal Gardens at Vauxhall, which was a very popular place of entertainment.

'The young ladies must have a gentleman each,' said Amelia's father. 'Jos will forget all about Emmy if he's looking after Miss Sharp. Ask George Osborne if he'll come.'

He and his wife exchanged little smiles, and Amelia looked down and blushed as only a young girl of seventeen can blush – and as Miss Rebecca Sharp had never blushed in her life.

But on the night of the Vauxhall party, it rained heavily, and the young people had to postpone their excursion. They spent a comfortable evening at home instead. The Sedleys had known George Osborne all his life, and it was accepted in both families that he and Amelia would marry one day. In fact, the marriage settlement had already been agreed between the two fathers.

So it was a very informal evening, and when Amelia and George went off to the piano in the back drawing-room, Becky and Joseph were left alone. Joseph was surprised to find that he could talk to Becky quite easily. She asked him many questions about India and listened admiringly to all his stories.

'Promise me that you will never go on one of those dreadful tiger hunts,' she begged him, her green eyes filled with fear.

Joseph laughed bravely. 'Nonsense, Miss Sharp. The danger only makes it more exciting.' He had only once been on a tiger hunt, when he had indeed nearly died – of terror.

Later, Rebecca, whose singing was as excellent as her French, sang a song about an orphan, her voice trembling a little over the sad ending. Everyone was reminded of Rebecca's own orphan state and her uncertain future in life.

'Such a beautiful song, dear Miss Sharp,' said Joseph Sedley. 'It almost made me cry.'

'That's because you have a kind heart, Mr Joseph,' came the soft reply, accompanied by an even softer glance.

Becky's efforts were not wasted. Joseph's mind was full of thoughts of marriage. 'She'll make a fine little wife,' he said to himself. 'I'll ask the question at Vauxhall. Yes, I will!'

✢

George Osborne came to lunch on the day of the Vauxhall party and said to Mrs Sedley, 'I hope you don't mind, but I've asked Dobbin to come here tonight and go with us to Vauxhall.'

Lieutenant George Osborne and Captain William Dobbin had been at school together. Dobbin, a quiet, modest boy, had saved Osborne from a beating, and from then on the two had been good friends. They were now both in the same regiment in the army and had not long returned from service in the West Indies.

'Of course he can come,' said Mrs Sedley. 'I remember Dobbin very well. Is he still as awkward and plain as ever?'

'I'll always like him,' Amelia said, 'however awkward he is.' But her reason for liking Dobbin was that he was George's friend.

'He's a fine fellow,' said George, 'even if he's not very good-looking.' And he glanced towards the mirror, admiring his own handsome face and curly black hair. He blushed a little when he saw Rebecca watching him, and Rebecca thought, 'And you certainly know what a fine fellow *you* are, don't you!'

That evening, when Amelia came into the sitting-room, singing happily, and as fresh as a rose in a pretty white dress, a very tall awkward gentleman in uniform stepped forward. He had large hands and feet, and bowed clumsily.

He had arrived very quietly, and the ladies upstairs did not know that he was there. Otherwise Amelia would not have come into the room singing. As it was, the fresh little voice went straight to William Dobbin's heart – and stayed there. 'What a lucky fellow George Osborne is,' he thought.

On the way to Vauxhall Gardens, Rebecca sat next to Joseph in the carriage and George Osborne sat between Amelia and Dobbin. Though nothing was said, everybody in the carriage was sure that Joseph would propose to Becky that evening. And when they stepped down from the carriage, Joseph took her on his arm, and George and Amelia went off together.

Dobbin paid for them all, and then walked behind, content

in his generous and unselfish way to see Amelia and George so happy together. They had all promised to stay together, but within ten minutes, of course, they had separated, and Rebecca found herself alone with Joseph on one of the side walks. Now, she thought, was the moment for Joseph to ask the question. A few minutes earlier somebody had rudely pushed past Rebecca, and she had fallen back with a little cry, into Mr Sedley's arms. This made him feel very loving towards her, and he told her several of his Indian stories again – for the sixth time.

'How I should like to see India!' breathed Rebecca.

'Would you really?' Joseph asked eagerly, and the important question must have been trembling on his lips, because he was breathing very heavily. Rebecca placed her little hand on his heart and she could feel it beating wildly.

Just at this interesting moment, however, the bell rang for the start of the fireworks, and the lovers were surrounded by crowds of hurrying people, and were forced to go with them.

Captain Dobbin walked round the Gardens alone. He thought of joining the others for supper, but saw, when he passed in front of their table, that they were all talking happily to each other, and that their table was prepared for four only. They had forgotten all about him, so he went away again. When he returned later, he realized that Joseph had drunk too much, for he was talking and laughing and singing very loudly. He had attracted a crowd of people, who were gathering round to watch. In fact, George was just about to hit one man who wanted to join the party, but Dobbin arrived at that moment and sent the crowd away.

'Good Heavens! Where *have* you been, Dobbin?' said George. Then, without waiting for a reply, he added, 'Make yourself useful. Look after Joseph, and I'll take the ladies home.'

That night as she went up to bed, Rebecca said to herself, 'He must propose tomorrow. He called me his darling four times. He *must* propose tomorrow.'

George was about to hit one man who wanted to join the party.

But wine can be the ruin of marriage plans. The next day Joseph had a terrible headache, and his condition was not improved by a visit from George Osborne, who laughed at him most unkindly. 'What a fool you made of yourself last night, Jos! Singing love songs, and crying all over Miss Sharp's hand!'

George had been thinking about Joseph and Becky Sharp. If he, George, was going to marry into the Sedley family, he did not want his brother-in-law to marry a governess, a little nobody, without money or social position. And so George continued to laugh at Joseph and make cruel jokes about him.

The result of all this was that Joseph decided that he was too ill to visit the young ladies, and the next day he sent a letter to his sister, saying that when he recovered he planned to go to Scotland for several months.

It was the death of Rebecca's hopes. Kind-hearted Amelia was very sad for her friend and cried a great deal, but it was now clear to the rest of the Sedley family that the time had come for Rebecca to leave. She made her preparations, and accepted all Amelia's parting gifts with just the right amount of hesitation. Even George Osborne gave Rebecca a present, but he had made too many unkind jokes about Joseph and the Vauxhall party.

'I'm so grateful to him!' Rebecca told Amelia, but in her heart she was thinking, 'George Osborne prevented my marriage.' So we can imagine just how grateful she was to George Osborne.

And so the final parting came. After many tears and promises of undying friendship, both sincere and insincere, Rebecca and Amelia said goodbye.

2

Becky Sharp makes new friends

Becky Sharp left London and travelled down to Queen's Crawley in Hampshire, the home of Sir Pitt Crawley. Sir Pitt was a baronet and a Member of Parliament, and the land-owning Crawley family was of a higher social class than the Sedleys and the Osbornes, who had made their money by commerce. This thought comforted Becky as she reflected on her failed adventure with Mr Joseph Sedley.

After a week Amelia received a letter from her friend.

MY DEAREST, SWEETEST AMELIA – Oh, how my life has changed from those happy times in your house! There I was surrounded by the kindness of a loving friend, and now . . .!

Sir Pitt Crawley is nothing like we silly girls imagined a baronet to be. Think of a short old man, in dirty old clothes, who smokes a horrible pipe, speaks with a rough uneducated accent, swears at his servants, and gets drunk every night! He has been married twice, I learn, and has two sons by his first wife. The older, Mr Pitt Crawley, still lives here. He's a pale, thin, ugly man, who is always reading religious books and riding around the countryside, telling everybody to lead good lives.

As for Lady Crawley, Sir Pitt's second wife, she is a poor, faded, unhappy creature, who has nothing to say. She is quite often ill, and spends the rest of her time sewing. I am governess to her two little girls, Rose and Violet, who are no trouble, and already love me quite as much as their mother, I think!

Sir Pitt also has a brother, Mr Bute Crawley. He and his wife, whom everyone calls Mrs Bute (there are so many Crawleys!), live in a house nearby. It seems that he and Sir Pitt don't get on – some quarrel about money, I believe. Indeed, Sir Pitt himself is very mean – I am not allowed to have a candle in my room after eleven at night! But of course I cannot complain, as I am only a poor little governess!

Your affectionate friend, Rebecca

Becky may have been a poor governess, but she was a clever, cunning little creature as well. For we must remember that this story has *Vanity Fair* for a title, and Vanity Fair is a very vain, wicked, foolish place, full of all sorts of falseness and pretence.

It was certainly true that Sir Pitt Crawley was a mean, selfish, rude old man. He was never known to give away a penny, or to do a good action, but he enjoyed a joke – and the company of a lively and amusing young woman. So the little governess had no difficulty in making herself useful and agreeable to her employer. She wrote his letters for him, played cards with him, and helped with the management of the farm, park and gardens.

Before many months had passed she was almost mistress of the house, though she was always careful to appear modest and respectful. She was popular with everyone, it seemed, including two other members of the Crawley family, whom she described in another letter to her dear friend.

PLEASE FORGIVE MY LONG SILENCE, dearest Amelia, but for some weeks now our usual quiet life at Queen's Crawley has been quite different, because Miss Matilda Crawley is here on her yearly visit. We have dinner-parties and dancing-parties; we drink the best wines every day, and there are fires in every room. Miss Crawley, you see, is Sir Pitt's unmarried half-sister. She is a fat old lady, but has a fortune of seventy thousand pounds, which makes her brothers, Sir Pitt and Mr Bute, very affectionate towards her, as you might imagine! It is said that she intends to divide her fortune between Mr Bute's family, and Sir Pitt's younger son, Rawdon Crawley, who is a captain in the army and a great favourite with his aunt. This Captain Rawdon is staying here now, and I suppose you will like to know what sort of person he is.

Well, he is a very large, fashionable young man. He has a loud voice, swears a great deal, and is always giving orders to the servants, who all love him in spite of this, for he is very generous with his money – when he has any! He leads quite a wild life, I believe, gambling and so on, but his aunt Miss Matilda just laughs, and often pays his debts for him. She says he is worth far more than his boring brother, Mr Pitt Crawley, whom she hates.

Shall I tell you a compliment Captain Rawdon paid me? One night at a dancing-party he asked me, the poor little governess, to dance with him, and afterwards he swore out loud that I was the neatest little dancer in the room. You should have seen the angry stares I received from all the fine young ladies!

Your affectionate friend, Rebecca

Becky did not, strange to say, give her dear friend an altogether accurate report of Captain Rawdon Crawley. The Captain had paid her not just one, but a great many compliments. The Captain had walked with her twenty times in the park, had met her in fifty corridors and passages. The Captain had leaned over her piano

'I am governess,' Becky wrote to Amelia, 'to Lady Crawley's two little girls, who are no trouble . . .'

in the evenings as she sang, while Miss Matilda Crawley nodded sleepily in her chair by the fire. (Lady Crawley was now upstairs, being ill, and ignored by everyone in the house.)

Nor did Becky mention to her friend what a great liking Miss Crawley had taken to her. Nothing would satisfy the old lady but that Miss Sharp should always sit next to her at dinner, and entertain her with amusing conversation.

'You've more brains in your little finger, my dear, than most people have in their heads,' she said to Becky. 'You're certainly cleverer than my poor nephew Rawdon.'

And so, in truth, she was – cleverer than both father and son.

🙊

Not long after this, a carriage stopped at Miss Matilda Crawley's home in London in Park Lane, a fine comfortable house, and Miss Crawley herself was carried inside. Doctors were called, and the old lady was put to bed and cared for day and night by a young person who had accompanied her from Queen's Crawley. No one else was allowed in the sickroom, and this was naturally very upsetting to Miss Briggs, who had been Miss Crawley's devoted companion and friend for many years.

This mysterious young person was none other, of course, than Miss Rebecca Sharp. She nursed Miss Crawley, gave orders to the servants, and very soon persuaded kind-hearted Miss Briggs into friendly feelings towards her.

Captain Rawdon Crawley visited every day, and spent a good deal of time in the company of Miss Sharp, receiving reports about his aunt's health. This improved rapidly, her illness being caused by no more than a rather large, hot fish supper, but when an old lady of great wealth becomes ill, all her affectionate relations are naturally anxious to pay her every attention.

It was not the same case for another member of the Crawley family, however. Sir Pitt's wife, Lady Crawley, had been ill for some time but no one had paid her any attention at all. And some three months after Becky had gone to London, Lady Crawley quietly slipped out of this life, almost unnoticed.

Sir Pitt had missed Becky greatly. It was only his fear of offending his wealthy sister that had made him let Becky go to London at all. He had written to her several times and often visited her in Park Lane, begging her, commanding her to return and continue the education of his two daughters. But Miss Crawley always refused to let her go, and so Becky stayed.

The day after Lady Crawley's death, Sir Pitt appeared in Park Lane. Miss Crawley did not want to see him, so she sent Becky down with a message that she was too ill to have visitors.

'That's all right,' Sir Pitt said. 'It's you I want to see, Miss Becky. I want you back at Queen's Crawley. It's not the same without you. All my accounts have got confused again. I can't get my letters done. You *must* come back. Dear Becky, do come.'

'I don't think – it would be right – to be alone – with you, sir,' said Becky, seeming rather upset.

'Come as Lady Crawley, if you like,' the baronet said. 'There! Will that satisfy you? Come back and be my wife. Yes or no?'

Tears ran down Becky's face, tears of real sorrow.

'Oh, Sir Pitt!' she said. 'Oh, Sir – I – I'm married already!'

'Married!' cried Sir Pitt. 'Married! Who to? You're joking. Who would marry you, Becky? You've not a penny to your name!'

Becky fell to her knees. 'Oh, Sir Pitt, dear Sir Pitt, please don't be angry. I'm so grateful for all your goodness to me.'

'Grateful be damned!' shouted Sir Pitt. 'Where is this husband, then? Run off and left you, has he?'

16

'Oh, sir! Please let me come back to dear Queen's Crawley. I can't be your wife, sir. Let me – let me be your daughter!'

At this moment the door opened, and Miss Crawley walked in.

Miss Briggs, accidentally listening at the door, had heard Sir Pitt's proposal and had rushed upstairs to tell Miss Crawley. Neither of them, however, had heard Becky's reason for refusing Sir Pitt's offer of marriage.

'Can this be true, Sir Pitt?' Miss Crawley asked, in a horrified voice. 'You have actually proposed marriage to Miss Sharp?'

'I have told Sir Pitt,' said Becky, in a sad, tearful voice, 'that I can never become Lady Crawley.'

'You've refused him!' said Miss Crawley, amazed that a penniless governess should refuse a baronet. 'But why? Is there someone else?'

'I cannot tell you now,' replied poor Becky. 'I am very miserable. But oh, promise you will love me always.'

Pleased that Rebecca had shown the good sense to refuse Sir Pitt, Miss Crawley promised always to remain Rebecca's friend. To Becky's relief, finding his offer of marriage refused, Sir Pitt left, without revealing her secret to Miss Crawley. So Becky had time to make plans, and that night she sat down and wrote a letter to a certain Miss Eliza Styles.

DEAREST FRIEND – The crisis we have talked about so often has arrived! Half of my secret is known. Sir Pitt came today and asked me – to marry him! Think of that! He knows that I am married, but not to whom. Now is the moment to tell Miss Crawley the truth. But she likes me, and she will forgive you anything. So, all will be well. She will die and leave us all her money, and you will stop gambling, and be a good boy. R.

Miss Eliza Styles was, of course, no other than Captain Rawdon Crawley. That big, handsome soldier had become so devoted to little Rebecca that there was no solution but to marry her. He admired her tremendously, believing her to be the cleverest little thing alive, and when he received her orders to rent some rooms for their new home, he hurried at once to obey.

That night in Park Lane, Becky was especially charming to Miss Crawley and Miss Briggs. And after the business with Sir Pitt, Becky, with her secret sorrows, was the heroine of the day.

On the second day after Sir Pitt's proposal the servant went to wake Miss Sharp as usual, but almost at once ran to Miss Briggs's room in great excitement.

'Oh, Miss Briggs,' said the servant, 'Miss Sharp's bed hasn't been slept in. And I found this letter for you in her room.'

'*What!*' cried Miss Briggs. She opened the letter eagerly.

DEAR, KIND MISS BRIGGS – I know that you will pity me and forgive me. I must leave the home where I have known nothing but kindness. I must do my duty and go to my husband, who commands me to join him. Yes, I am married, married to the best and most generous of men – Captain Rawdon Crawley!

Only you, dear Miss Briggs, will know how to give this news to his devoted aunt. Tell her how much it hurts me to leave her. Ask her to forgive the poor girl to whom she has shown such affection. Ask Miss Crawley to forgive her children.

Your affectionate and grateful Rebecca Crawley

As Miss Briggs finished reading the letter, the servant came to tell her that Mrs Bute Crawley had arrived from Hampshire. Mrs Bute was a strong and determined woman, and she and her husband, Sir Pitt's brother, were anxious to pay Miss Crawley every attention. Like Rawdon, they too were in debt and their hopes lay in Miss Crawley's death, since they expected a good share of her money.

Still holding the letter, Miss Briggs ran downstairs to tell Mrs Bute the terrible, shocking news of the marriage.

'It's a good thing I'm here,' said Mrs Bute, 'to take care of poor, dear Miss Crawley. But at least it will open her eyes to that girl. I always knew she was a wicked, cunning little thing.'

Mrs Bute and Miss Briggs waited until Miss Crawley was downstairs, seated comfortably in her armchair. And then they began to prepare her for the dreadful news about Rebecca.

'There was a reason for her refusing Sir Pitt,' said Mrs Bute.

'Of course there was a reason,' Miss Crawley answered. 'She likes someone else.'

'*Likes*!' Miss Briggs gasped. 'Oh, my dear Miss Crawley, she is married already!'

'The secretive little creature! How dare she not tell me!' cried Miss Crawley. 'Send her to me at once!'

'We cannot,' said Mrs Bute. 'Oh, prepare yourself, dear friend! Miss Sharp has – gone!'

'She went last night,' Miss Briggs said. 'She left a letter for me. She's married to—'

'Such shocking news! Oh, do tell her gently!' said Mrs Bute.

'Married to whom?' said Miss Crawley, in a nervous fury.

'To – to a relation of—' Miss Briggs could not continue.

'Tell me!' cried Miss Crawley. 'Don't drive me mad!'

'Oh, Miss Crawley! She's married to your nephew Rawdon!'

'Rawdon – Rebecca – married! A governess! You stupid old fool, Briggs, I don't believe you!'

The old lady screamed in fury, then fell back in a faint, and had to be taken to bed. The doctor was sent for, and Mrs Bute went to sit by the bedside to act as nurse. 'Her relations ought to be round her at a time like this,' she said, full of concern.

No sooner had Miss Crawley been carried to her room than Sir Pitt arrived at the house. 'Where's Becky?' he said. 'Tell her to get her things together. She's coming with me to Queen's Crawley, even if she is married.'

'Haven't you heard the news?' cried Miss Briggs. 'She's gone. And she has married your son – Captain Rawdon!'

When Sir Pitt heard this news, he broke out into such furious language that it sent poor Miss Briggs trembling from the room. The old man went away, back to Queen's Crawley, and there we will leave him, wild with hatred and unsatisfied desire.

❧

'Suppose the old lady doesn't forgive us,' Rawdon said to his wife as they sat together in their comfortable little London home. He had filled it with presents for his wife – flowers, perfumes, a piano, jewellery, dresses . . . Becky had been trying her new piano all morning, and new rings sparkled on her little fingers. 'Suppose she doesn't forgive us, eh, Becky?'

'Then *I'll* make your fortune,' she said, patting his cheek.

'You can do anything,' her husband said, kissing her little hand. 'Come on, let's go out for dinner.'

Amelia Sedley nearly loses hope

And what has happened to Amelia Sedley during this time? While Rebecca was working so hard to make her future safe with the Crawley family, her dear friend Amelia had nothing to do but to sit in her comfortable home, with loving parents, and wait for George Osborne's visits.

Unfortunately, these visits were not at all frequent. George was often with his regiment down in Kent, and when he was in London, he seemed to have so many other things to do, so many friends to see, so many games of cards to play. Amelia saw more of his sisters, Miss Jane Osborne and Miss Maria Osborne, since the Osbornes' home was just the other side of Russell Square.

The two Miss Osbornes were rather proud young ladies. They did not think Amelia was good enough for their handsome brother, and they did not treat her kindly. 'What *can* George see in that dull little creature?' they asked each other.

So Amelia sat at home, waiting for George, and worrying about Napoleon Bonaparte and the talk of war. She had heard reports that George's regiment would be sent to France to fight Napoleon's army, and the thought terrified her. She asked Dobbin about it when he visited the Sedleys one day. No orders had yet been received, Dobbin told her gently. He was very upset to see Amelia so unhappy and so neglected by George.

Time went past and still George did not visit, but poor little soft-hearted Amelia went on hoping and trusting. She loved George Osborne with all her heart, and wrote to him every day – long, long letters, which were not very well written, but were full of love, devoted, uncritical, unquestioning love.

These letters became quite a joke with George's friends in the regiment. On one occasion George was seen lighting his cigar with one of them, to the horror of Captain Dobbin, who would have very much liked to receive such a letter himself. In fact, Dobbin was so angry that he could remain silent no longer.

'George,' he said, 'are you going to marry Amelia or not?'

'Is that any business of yours?' George asked fiercely.

'Yes, it is, George, because you're neglecting a sweet girl. You should have seen her sad little face when I visited the other day. Go and comfort her, you bad fellow, instead of spending all your time in gambling-houses when you're in town.'

'I'm very fond of Amelia, of course I am,' said George, 'but – but a man must enjoy himself before he gets married, you know.'

'Go and see her,' said Dobbin, 'or write her a long letter. Do something to make her happy. It won't take much.'

'You're right. Yes, I'll go tomorrow. It's true, she *is* very fond of me,' George said, in a self-satisfied way.

He did go to see Amelia the next day, and Dobbin even lent him some money to buy her a present. George probably would have done so, but on the way to the Sedleys' house, he saw a very nice diamond shirt-pin, and he bought it for himself.

When he arrived, Amelia's sad little face lit up in the sunshine of George's smile. She ran to him, and George kissed her fondly on the forehead and was very affectionate with her; and she thought his diamond shirt-pin (which she had not seen him wear before) was the prettiest thing ever seen.

Since George was only in town for one day, he invited Emmy
to dine with him at his father's house that evening, and took her
to spend the afternoon with his sisters while he went off to see

George was seen lighting his cigar with one of Amelia's letters,
to the horror of Captain Dobbin.

to some important business (trying on a new coat, and playing several games of billiards with a friend).

He was late home for dinner, and found his father in a very bad mood and his sisters and Amelia eating in nervous silence. When the ladies had gone up to the drawing-room, leaving father and son to their wine, George watched his father's face anxiously. He needed urgently to ask his father for money, to pay off some of his debts, but when he cautiously raised the subject, he did not get the explosion of bad temper he had feared.

'Well, well,' Mr Osborne said, 'young men will be young men. I know you're mixing in the best society, and I like to see it. You have to pay your own way, and my money's as good as theirs, George my boy. You can call at my bank tomorrow.'

George was relieved and properly grateful, but it seemed that the old gentleman had something else on his mind.

'That little girl upstairs – Amelia,' he said. 'What do you intend to do about her, George?'

'Well, it's clear, isn't it?' George said. 'She's very fond of me. Anyone can see that. And didn't you order me to marry her, and don't I always obey you?'

'Mmm,' said Mr Osborne. 'Pass the wine, boy. Why shouldn't you marry higher than just old Sedley's daughter, eh?'

'But you and Mr Sedley arranged this years ago,' said George.

'Things have changed since then,' his father said, frowning. 'Sedley's business is not doing well. I'm not sure that he can pay the money we agreed on for the marriage settlement. In fact, unless Sedley can pay me ten thousand pounds now, there will be no marriage between you and Amelia Sedley.'

George was especially good to Amelia that evening, and even visited her again the next morning on his way to his father's bank.

Later in the day Amelia, still anxious about old Mr Osborne's coldness to her the day before, wrote George another of her long letters – four pages of love and fear and hope and worry.

'Poor little Emmy – dear little Emmy! How fond she is of me,' George said, reading the letter after a lively evening with his friends. 'And oh Lord, what a headache this red wine has given me!' Poor little Emmy, indeed.

No more than four months later, Mr Osborne's words to his son were proved true. Old John Sedley was a ruined man. He had judged badly and lost money, and could not recover from his mistakes. The final disaster struck when Napoleon escaped from the island of Elba and invaded France. The money market crashed, taking with it what remained of Mr Sedley's fortune. The family had to leave their fine home in Russell Square, and all the contents of the house were put up for sale.

On the day of the sale, who should visit the house in Russell Square but our old friends, Captain and Mrs Rawdon Crawley? Rebecca had seen her dear friend Amelia a few times since she had been at Miss Crawley's house. Amelia and George Osborne visited her, and Rawdon invited George several times to little gambling parties, which George always accepted, happy to lose money to the son of a baronet and his high-society friends.

About a month after Becky had set up home with Rawdon, she expressed a wish to see Amelia again. Money being short in the Crawleys' little home, and with no sign of forgiveness from Miss Crawley, Rawdon agreed that it would be good to see George Osborne again. 'I'd like to play a few more games of cards with him. He'd be what I call *useful* just now,' he said, with his loud soldier's laugh. Rawdon Crawley had no intention of cheating George Osborne, of course; it was just rather convenient to gamble with someone less skilful than himself.

When they arrived in Russell Square, Rebecca was shocked to see a sale at the house where she had once been treated so kindly. However, this did not stop her from trying to buy Amelia's piano, though it is not clear why she wanted it. Perhaps her own piano had been sold in order to pay the rent.

But the piano was finally sold to Captain Dobbin, who knew how much Amelia loved her piano and who paid a great deal more for it than the piano was worth. Rebecca and Rawdon looked for him after the sale, hoping to find out more about what had caused the Sedleys' ruin, but he had already left.

'I'm sorry Mr Sedley has had such bad luck,' Becky said as they got back into their carriage. 'He was a very kind old man.'

'Oh, it happens all the time with businessmen, you know,' Rawdon said. 'I don't suppose Osborne will marry your pretty little friend now. How upset she'll be, hey, Becky?'

'Oh, I expect she'll recover,' Becky said with a smile, and they drove on and talked about something else.

The news of Sedley's ruin was announced in the newspaper, and soon became widely known. The family moved to a little house in an unfashionable street. Mr Sedley's former friends now avoided him, but what really hurt him was that his most bitter, most unforgiving enemy was John Osborne, George's father, whom Sedley had helped many years before, when Osborne was starting his own business.

In a short, cruel letter, Mr Osborne informed Amelia that her father's behaviour had been so shameful that there could be no marriage between her and his son. Amelia accepted the news almost as if she had been expecting it. For some time, she had suspected that George no longer loved her, although in her heart she wanted to go on believing that he did. She showed little emotion outwardly, but alone in her little room in the new house, that gentle heart quietly died a little more each day.

As for John Sedley, he spoke of the Osbornes with bitterness and anger, and swore that nothing on earth would persuade him to allow his daughter to marry John Osborne's son. He ordered Amelia to put George Osborne from her mind and to return all his gifts and letters. The poor girl tried to obey him, and put together a few of George's little gifts. She took out his letters and read them all again, but how could she return them? How could she put George from her mind? And she put the letters back in their secret place, to read later, over and over again.

Meanwhile, Napoleon was marching into Paris, and the British Army, including of course the regiment in which George and Dobbin served, was ordered abroad to join the fighting.

When Dobbin heard the news, his first thought was for Amelia, knowing how this would add to her sorrows. George, however, felt nothing but excitement. He had just been made a captain, and he was enjoying trying on his fine new uniform. That evening he went to see his father, who told him again that there could be no marriage with Amelia – and gave George a large amount of money to pay for his new clothes. Money was always useful to George, and he took it without many words. On the way back from his father's house, he passed the Sedleys' old home, now closed up. Where were the Sedleys now? The thought of their ruin made George sad.

Three days later, Dobbin found George looking miserable.

'She – she's sent me back some things I gave her,' he said, and he showed Dobbin the letter Amelia had sent.

MY FATHER HAS ordered me to return these presents to you, and this is the last time I may write to you. I am sure you are as unhappy as I am that we cannot marry, and I do not blame you in any way. I am sure you had nothing to do with the cruel things which Mr Osborne has said. Goodbye. I pray that I may be strong enough to bear this. I shall often play upon the piano – your piano. It was so kind of you to send it. Amelia

Dobbin was very soft-hearted. The idea of Amelia so lonely and unhappy made him break out into a passion of praise for her. George listened, remembering Amelia's sweetness, her unquestioning love for him, and thought about what he had lost.

'Where are they?' he asked, ashamed that he had made no effort to find Amelia. 'There's no address in the letter.'

Dobbin knew where they were. Had he not sent the piano there? In fact, he had visited Mrs Sedley and Amelia the day before, and been shocked by Amelia's pale face and lifeless eyes. It was he who had brought the packet back for George.

'How is she? How did she look?' asked George.

'George, she's dying,' William Dobbin said.

Four hours after the talk between Dobbin and Osborne, the Sedleys' little servant girl came into Amelia's room. As usual, Amelia was sitting reading her old love letters from George.

'Miss Emmy,' said the girl. 'There's someone – look, here's a message.' She gave her a letter, which Amelia opened and read.

I must see you. Dearest Emmy – dearest wife, come to me.

George and her mother were outside, waiting until she had read the letter, and a minute later the door was thrown open.

A harder heart than George's would have melted at the sight of that sweet face, that flood of despairing tears as Amelia wept over his hand, kissing it again and again. Full of emotion at the sight of so grateful and devoted a slave, George swore to himself that he would make her happy, no matter what happened.

Overnight, Amelia became her old self again, bright-eyed and cheerful, full of smiles and laughter, and eagerly waiting for George's next visit. She smiled at Captain Dobbin, who usually came with George, but apart from that she did not notice him.

Dobbin, though sad at heart, was content. He believed Amelia would only be happy if she married George, and so he was determined to make that happen. He urged George to speak to his father, and to persuade him to agree to the marriage.

But that fierce old gentleman had other plans, and had his eye on an extremely wealthy young lady as a bride for his son.

The storm broke one night at dinner. The name of Amelia Sedley, forbidden by the father, was spoken by the son. 'She's the best, the gentlest, the sweetest girl in England,' said George.

'George!' said Jane Osborne, glancing in alarm at their father.

But George did not lack courage, and stared back at his father coolly. As soon as they could, his sisters hurried away to the drawing-room, leaving father and son to their battle.

'How dare you, sir, mention that person's name in my house?' demanded old Mr Osborne, his face purple with fury.

'Stop, sir. You don't use the word "dare" to a captain in the British Army,' said George.

'I shall say what I like to my son, sir. I can cut him off with a penny if I like. I can make him a beggar if I like. I *will* say what I like,' his father said. 'No gentleman, not even a fine captain in the British Army, has the right to insult his father.'

'I never insulted you, sir,' George said. 'But I shall defend Miss Sedley and her name wherever I go.'

'That name is forbidden in this house!' screamed his father.

'Who told me to love her?' demanded George. 'I might have chosen elsewhere, but I obeyed you. And now that her heart is mine, you order me to throw it away, to punish her for the faults of other people. Well, sir, I won't do it!'

'I won't have this damned nonsense, sir. If you choose to throw away eight thousand pounds a year, you may do it, but by God you will walk out of this house, sir, and not come back.'

And with that, Mr Osborne shouted for a servant and ordered him to call a carriage for Captain Osborne.

An hour later in the army camp George, looking very pale, went to find Dobbin. 'I've done it,' he said.

'Done what?' asked Dobbin.

George told him. 'And I'll marry Amelia tomorrow,' he said. 'I love her more every day, Dobbin.'

And so, quietly and secretly, George Osborne and Amelia Sedley were married, to the sound of rain beating down on the church roof, and Mrs Sedley crying quietly. Captain Dobbin arranged the wedding, and as old Mr Sedley refused to have anything to do with it, Amelia's brother Joseph came to give away the bride.

When the ceremony was over and the kissing and the hand-shaking were all done, the happy couple drove away in Joseph's carriage. Captain Dobbin stood outside the church and watched them go. Never in his life had he felt so miserable and lonely. Then he turned and walked away, through the rain.

4

A pleasant stay in Brighton

Seven days after the wedding, three young men were walking by the sea in Brighton, enjoying the sea air and admiring all the pretty ladies as they passed.

'There's a fine girl over there,' said one of the three. 'D'you see? A very pretty ankle, she's got.'

'You're a devil for the ladies, Jos!' laughed one of his friends. 'But what shall we do this afternoon, boys?'

'Let's have a game of billiards,' said the third man.

'No, no, Captain,' said Jos, alarmed. 'No billiards today, Crawley, my boy; yesterday was enough.'

'You play very well,' laughed Crawley. 'Doesn't he, George?'

George Osborne had brought Amelia to Brighton for a little honeymoon, and Joseph Sedley had come down to join them. And who should they discover, staying in the same hotel, but Captain and Mrs Rawdon Crawley? At once Rebecca and Amelia flew into each other's arms, and there was general delight among the young people. The two wedding parties met constantly, on excursions and at dinners, and the gentlemen for games of cards and billiards, which conveniently enabled Rawdon to refill his empty purse with his winnings from Jos and George.

The two young couples had plenty to tell each other, and their marriages and future hopes were discussed with great interest on both sides. George was rather nervously waiting for the arrival of his friend Captain Dobbin, who had offered to tell George's father the news of his son's marriage to Amelia.

Miss Crawley, on whom all Rawdon's hopes depended, still refused to see him, and was now in Brighton, taking the sea air for her health. Her affectionate nephew and niece had followed her there, but Miss Crawley was guarded day and night by the fiercely possessive Mrs Bute Crawley, who was determined to prevent Rawdon inheriting any of his aunt's riches. Becky and Rawdon, however, were just as determined to succeed as Mrs Bute; and in the meantime they spent money freely and ran up debts, confident of getting the old lady's money in the end.

On meeting George Osborne again, Becky had taken some care to be especially charming to him, admiring his handsome face and his skill at billiards (at which he usually lost to Rawdon). In return, George thought Becky clever, amusing, stylish, and altogether delightful. He quite forgot his original opinion of her as a lowly governess.

Amelia became faintly uneasy about her brilliant friend, always so lively and amusing, while she herself was so shy and quiet. She had only been married a week, and already George seemed bored, eager to be with other people as much as possible.

It is hard for a young bride to have thoughts like these, but so it was. One evening, while Rawdon and Joseph were playing cards, Becky and George were outside on the balcony, admiring the moonlight. Amelia sat inside, neglected, watching.

'What a fine night!' said George. 'Do you mind my cigar?'

'Not a bit. I love the smell of them in the open air,' Becky said.

'The sea is so calm and clear – don't you wish you could just dive into it?' said George.

Becky laughed. 'Do you know what my plan is?' she said. 'You

*Amelia sat inside, neglected, watching Becky and George
on the balcony.*

remember Briggs, my Aunt Crawley's companion? She goes sea-bathing a lot, and one day I'm going to dive in next to her and insist on immediate forgiveness, right there in the water.'

George burst out laughing at the idea of this watery meeting.

'What's the noise about, you two?' Rawdon called out.

Amelia, unable to join in the laughter, crept away to her room, and a little cold hand closed around that tender heart.

But apart from these little private worries of Amelia's, the time passed pleasantly enough, and hopes on both sides were high – that George's father would forgive George, and that Miss Crawley would forgive Becky and Rawdon.

But Vanity Fair is rarely a kind or forgiving place. And what would happen to our story, dear reader, if it was?

The next day Dobbin arrived in Brighton, eager to see Amelia, even though she was now a married woman, forever out of his reach. He brought two pieces of news with him; the first he gave to the young men alone. It was news of war.

'We're ordered to Belgium – the whole army. We leave next week, sailing from Chatham.'

This news shocked his listeners, and they looked very serious.

'It's my opinion,' Dobbin went on, 'that Napoleon will attack in less than three weeks, and we shall have a fine old time of it. But let's not say anything like that to the ladies, George, eh? It may come to nothing after all – at the moment Brussels is full of fashionable people who think just that.'

The second piece of news Dobbin brought was for George Osborne, and he waited until they were alone together.

'What did my father say?' George asked anxiously. 'Tell me!'

Dobbin did not reply and silently handed George a letter.

'It's not in my father's handwriting,' said George, alarmed.
George was right. The letter was from his father's lawyer.

SIR – I AM INSTRUCTED by Mr Osborne to inform you that, as a
result of the marriage you have chosen to enter into, he no longer
recognizes you as his son, and that you will therefore inherit no
money from him on his death. The only inheritance due to you is
the money left to you and your two sisters by your mother. The
sum of £2000, being a third share of £6000, will be paid to yourself
or your agents upon receipt of your instructions.

Mr Osborne also asks me to say that he refuses to receive any
messages or letters from you on this or any other subject.

Your obedient servant, Samuel Higgs

'This is all your fault!' shouted George. He threw the letter
at Dobbin. 'We could have waited, but no – you had to get me
married, and ruined! What the devil am I to do with two thousand
pounds? That won't last me two years. I've already lost a hundred
and forty to Crawley at cards and billiards this week.'

'Well, yes, it's hard,' Dobbin said, 'and, as you say, it's partly
my fault, but there are some men who wouldn't mind changing
with you. You have more money than most of them. You must
live on your pay until your father changes his mind.'

'How can a man like me live on a soldier's pay?' George
shouted angrily. 'You're a fool, Dobbin. I *must* have my
comforts, keep up my position in the world. Do you expect my
wife to follow the regiment on foot, carrying her own luggage?'

'Well, well,' said Dobbin calmly. 'This storm will pass,
George. Get your name mentioned in the Army Gazette and I'm
sure your old father will welcome you back with open arms.'

'Mentioned in the Gazette!' said George. 'Among the list of dead, you mean? That's really helpful!'

'Don't talk like that,' said Dobbin. 'Everything will be fine.'

It was impossible to argue with Dobbin for long as he was too good-natured. He had tried his best for his friend, but the father was a man of violent temper, and having decided to cut his son off, there was nothing Dobbin, or George's two sisters, or anyone else could say to persuade him otherwise.

Before dinner that evening there were two little conversations between the husbands and wives in the hotel.

George gave Amelia the lawyer's letter. 'It's not myself I care about, Emmy,' he said, 'it's you.'

Amelia read the letter and her face cleared. The idea of being poor with the man she loved held no fears for her.

'Oh, George,' she said, 'I'm sure he will forgive you soon, but it's so sad for you to be separated from your father like this.'

'It is,' said George, looking deeply miserable. 'But you, my dear girl – my wife has the right to expect certain comforts, not the poor life of an ordinary army wife.'

'But, George,' said Amelia happily. 'I can sew, and mend your trousers for you, and do all kinds of things. And two thousand pounds is a great deal of money, isn't it, George?'

George had to laugh at this, and they went down to dinner.

In another room, Becky and Rawdon also talked about money.

'We'll all be leaving soon,' Becky said. 'Rawdon dear, you'd better get that money Osborne owes you before he goes.'

'Good idea,' said Rawdon. 'Wonder what Mrs O. will do when Osborne goes out to Brussels with the regiment?'

'Cry her eyes out, I expect,' said Becky.

'*You* won't cry about *me*, I suppose,' Rawdon said, half angry.

'You idiot!' said his wife. 'I'm coming with you, of course.'

At dinner that evening they were all very bright and cheerful. George was excited by the thought of war, and Dobbin told amusing stories, but when Brussels was mentioned, a look of terror came over Amelia's sweet, smiling face.

'Has the regiment been ordered to Brussels, George?' she cried. And she seized George's arm in her terror.

'Don't be afraid, Emmy,' said George. 'You can come too.'

'*I* intend to go,' said Rebecca. 'I must – General Tufto is a great admirer of mine. Isn't he, Rawdon?'

Rawdon gave his usual great roar of laughter.

'I must and will go,' cried Amelia, with great determination.

'Bravo!' said George, laughing. 'Did you ever see such a fierce little fighter of a wife?' he asked the others.

Dobbin disapproved strongly of Amelia being allowed to go anywhere near a possible battle, but of course he could not say that to her husband. 'At least,' he thought, 'I shall be able to see her, and I will be there to protect her and keep her safe.'

After dinner, the men stayed to smoke their cigars, then went to rejoin the ladies. Rawdon touched George on the arm.

'I say, Osborne,' he said lightly, 'could you let me have that small amount, if convenient?'

It was not at all convenient, but gambling debts must be paid, so a good many bank-notes passed from George to Rawdon.

The next day Jos, Dobbin, Amelia, and George left for London, to prepare for Brussels. Rawdon and Becky would follow in a few days. Becky and Amelia kissed each other most affectionately on parting, but a tiny flame of jealousy was already burning in Amelia's gentle heart.

Before Becky and Rawdon left Brighton, they carried out a last attack on Miss Crawley's defences. Becky had obtained the very useful information that Mr Bute Crawley had broken his collar-bone falling from his horse, and Mrs Bute had had to hurry home to look after him. That left Miss Briggs. Becky arranged to meet that lady by chance on the beach, and poured out declarations of love and affection and concern for Miss Crawley and herself. Miss Briggs, by nature a kindly person, was soon won round, and Becky hurried back to Rawdon in the hotel.

'You must sit down and write to your aunt at once, Rawdon,' she said. 'And then Briggs will try to persuade her to see you.'

'But what shall I write?' asked the puzzled Rawdon.

'Idiot,' said his wife, pulling his ear. 'I'll tell you what to say.'

And so she did, leaning over his shoulder to correct his spelling and grammar. The letter was in short, soldierly sentences, full of grateful affection, and made no mention of money.

Old Miss Crawley laughed when the letter arrived, and laughed even more when Miss Briggs had read it out to her.

'Rawdon never wrote a word of that letter,' she said. 'He never wrote to me without asking for money in his life, and all his letters are full of bad spelling and bad grammar. It's that little snake of a governess who rules him.' They are all the same, Miss Crawley thought in her heart. They all want me dead, and are hoping for my money. I wish they would all leave me alone.

She did agree to meet Rawdon briefly, but the interview was not a success, and that evening Rawdon received a letter from his aunt. Her health, she wrote, was too delicate for further meetings, but if he would like to call at her lawyer's office in London, he would find a communication waiting for him there.

At once, full of hope, Rawdon and Becky hurried back to

London (which was exactly Miss Crawley's intention), and the next day Rawdon went to the lawyer's. He came back furious.

'By God, Becky,' he said, 'she's only given me twenty pounds!'

Though it was against themselves, the joke was a good one, and Becky burst out laughing at Rawdon's angry face.

In London George also found that his financial future did not look promising. There was no sign that his father might forgive him, and when George went to collect his two thousand pounds from the lawyer, Mr Higgs was very cool and distant with him.

But George did not care. The old man would forgive him in the end, he thought, and as his army pay had gone in gambling losses to Captain Crawley, he began to spend his two thousand pounds. He took a large apartment in a fine hotel, entertained Jos and Dobbin to a very expensive dinner there (much to Dobbin's disapproval), and sent his wife out to buy a great many fashionable clothes, suitable for a grand social life in Brussels.

Amelia happily obeyed her husband's orders about shopping, but was a little sad when he would not go with her to visit her parents. Mrs Sedley wept with happiness to see her daughter, and Amelia found it oddly comforting to be with her kind old parents again. Only nine days married, and so much had changed! Did she admit to herself how different the real man was from that handsome hero she had adored before marriage? No, a man must be very bad indeed before a woman will admit such a thing, and whatever secret disappointments lay in that gentle heart, they stayed well hidden from the world.

Waiting for war in Brussels

Napoleon Bonaparte would be defeated, people said, almost without a struggle. Weren't the armies of Europe and the great Duke of Wellington lined up against him? Everyone had such perfect confidence in the result of the battle that the atmosphere in Brussels was one of pleasure and enjoyment. The city was full of fashionable English people, riding in the park, going to the opera, dancing and gambling the nights away.

Amelia was very happy for her first two weeks in Brussels. She was young and sweet-natured, and George's army friends thought she was 'a pretty little thing'. Everybody liked her and George himself was full of kind attention to his wife, buying her little gifts, and taking her out every night to a party or the opera.

Joseph, who had accompanied his sister to Brussels, was also enjoying himself. He was not a soldier, but since army men were the most popular in town, he grew a very fine military moustache, in order to look as much like an army officer as possible.

They first met the Crawleys again riding in the park. Rebecca was surrounded by admirers, and when Amelia saw her dear friend, her heart sank. The sun on that clear May day suddenly seemed to shine less brightly.

But George was delighted, riding over to shake Rawdon warmly by the hand.

'Good to see you, Crawley,' he said. 'How are you?'

George was full of kind attention to his wife, taking her out every night.

'All right, my boy,' said Rawdon. 'How's the business with your father? Has he given in?'

'Not yet,' said George. 'But he will. And I've some private fortune through my mother. What about your aunt?'

'Sent me twenty pounds, damned old woman. When shall we have a game, eh? Come round on Tuesday, why not?'

The Crawleys were at the opera that night as well. Becky was sitting in General Tufto's box, clearly a great favourite with the General, but as soon as she saw Amelia, she hurried round to see her. Such affectionate kisses! How was her dearest, best little Amelia? How pretty she was looking! And here was Mr Jos too, looking so well, and such a fine moustache! Becky smiled, and talked, and laughed, busily spreading charm all around her.

'What a slippery little snake that woman is!' honest old Dobbin murmured to George when Becky had left. 'She's acting all the time, didn't you see, George?'

'Acting? Nonsense! She's the nicest little woman in England,' George replied. 'You don't understand women, Dobbin.'

Dobbin understood enough about George, however, to become anxious after a few days, when he saw how often George was playing cards with Rawdon Crawley, and losing.

'When are you going to give up gambling, George?' he said.

'When are you going to give up criticizing me?' was the reply. 'Rawdon doesn't cheat, you know. I'll start winning some games soon – it all balances out in the end.'

'But I don't think Crawley could pay if he lost,' Dobbin said.

Good advice is never taken, and George continued to visit the Crawleys' hotel to play cards with Captain Crawley, and to attend the little dinners given by Mrs Crawley, whose green eyes always lit up when George came into the room – or so George liked to believe. In fact, he was convinced that Becky was in love with him, unable to resist such a handsome, charming fellow as himself. Meanwhile, Rawdon continued to beat him at cards.

George's gambling was the least of Amelia's worries. The more brilliantly Rebecca shone in society, the more shy and awkward Amelia became. The more time George spent in Rebecca's company, the more miserable and lonely Amelia became. But she said nothing, and suffered in secret.

In June there was a grand ball, to which George and Amelia, Dobbin, and the Crawleys were all invited. After generously buying his wife a new dress and some ornaments, George took her to the ball, where she did not know anyone, put her on a chair and left her there. She was free to amuse herself as she liked, but no one came to disturb her except Dobbin.

Amelia's appearance at the ball was a failure; Mrs Crawley's appearance, however, was a brilliant success. She arrived very late. Her eyes sparkled with life, her dress was perfection. At once there was a crowd of admirers around her, begging for a dance.

But Rebecca went straight to where poor little Amelia was sitting, and in the kindest possible way, began to criticize Amelia's dress, her hair, and her shoes.

'I'll send my own dressmaker to you tomorrow,' she said. 'And my dear,' she went on, 'do stop George from gambling. He and Rawdon play cards every night, and Rawdon will win every penny from him if he does not take care. Why don't you stop him, you careless girl? Oh, look, here comes your darling husband now.'

She turned to smile at George, who was approaching them.

'Where have you been, you wicked man?' she said. 'Here is Emmy crying her eyes out for you. Have you come to fetch me for our dance?'

43

And she left her shawl and her flowers by Amelia's side, and went away to dance with George. Only women know how to be so cruel. There is a poison on their sharp little knives which hurts far more than a man's blunter weapon.

Amelia sat alone with her sad thoughts in her corner, unnoticed except when Rawdon came to offer a few words of clumsy conversation, and when Dobbin brought her food and drink, and sat with her for a time.

At last George came back – for Rebecca's shawl and flowers. He took them away, but when he gave them back to their owner, there was a note, rolled up like a tiny snake among the flowers. Rebecca put out her hand to take them, and it was clear from her eyes that she knew what she would find there. She had been used to such notes from her early years. She gave him her hand and one of her quick, knowing glances, and George bowed over her hand, his heart hammering with the excitement of victory.

Amelia saw the glance, and suddenly it was too much.

'William,' she said to Dobbin, who was near her, 'you've always been kind to me – I'm – I'm not well. Take me home.'

He went away with her quickly. The streets seemed noisier and more crowded than usual, but the hotel was not far, and they soon reached it. Amelia went straight to bed.

George, meanwhile, wild with excitement, had been gambling and had then gone to spend his winnings on drink. Dobbin found him with a glass in his hand, and red in the face.

'Hallo, Dob! Come and drink, Dob!' George called out.

'Come away, George,' Dobbin said quietly. 'Don't drink.'

'Have a drink, old boy,' George said. 'Stop being so serious.'

Dobbin came close to George and whispered in his ear. At once George banged his glass down on the table and, taking his friend's arm, walked quickly away with him. 'The enemy has advanced,' Dobbin had said. 'The fighting has already begun. Come away – we march in three hours.'

❧

Back in his hotel, George thought about a thousand things – his past life – his chances in war – his wife – the child, perhaps, whom he might never see. Oh, how he wished that note to Becky had never been written, and that he could say goodbye without guilt to the gentle girl whose love he had valued so little!

He thought over his short married life. He had wasted all his money. Why had he been so wild and careless? If he was killed, what would be left for her? He was not good enough for her. Poor Emmy. He should never have married her. Why hadn't he obeyed his father, who had always been so generous to him?

Full of selfish regret, he sat down and wrote a last letter to his father. By the time he had finished, it was almost day. He went into the bedroom and looked down at Amelia's sweet, pale face. How pure and innocent she was, and how badly he had treated her! How selfish he was! Sick with shame, he watched the sleeping girl, then bent down to kiss that pale cheek.

Two pretty little arms closed gently round his neck. 'I am awake, George,' the poor girl said, her eyes full of tears.

And at that moment outside the window the bugles sounded, and the drums began to beat. The city was waking up to war.

❧

In another hotel the Crawleys were also saying their goodbyes. Rawdon truly loved Becky and had known real happiness in his marriage. He was anxious for the future, and much more affected by the parting than his brave little wife who, having wisely decided to be calm and sensible, tried to laugh away his fears.

45

'It's no laughing matter, Mrs Crawley,' her husband said, sounding hurt. 'I'm a big man, easy to shoot at. And if I drop, I want to be sure you'll be all right.'

Becky became serious at once. 'Dearest love,' she said softly, 'do you suppose I feel nothing?' She quickly wiped her eyes, then smiled lovingly at her husband.

'Now, let's see,' said Rawdon, comforted. 'I've had some luck at the card-tables, and here's two hundred and thirty pounds. I won't take my horses – I'll ride one of the General's. If I'm hit, you can sell them – should get a good price for them.'

And Rawdon Crawley, who had seldom thought about anyone but himself until these last few months, wrote down a list of all the things Rebecca could sell if he was killed. Then he put on his oldest uniform, leaving the best for Rebecca to sell, and before he left, he picked her up in his arms and held her close to his heart. His eyes were clouded, as he put her down and left her.

Rebecca waved goodbye to him from the window, and stood there for a moment looking out after he was gone. The sun was just rising as she turned away from the window, and saw on a table her flowers from the ball. She picked them up, and saw the little note pushed in between them. With a smile, she took the note out and locked it away in her little writing desk. Then she put the flowers in water, went to bed, and slept deeply.

It was ten o'clock when she woke, and after drinking her coffee, she continued Rawdon's list, adding to it all the gifts and jewellery she had received from her admirers. She was pleased to find that if her husband did not return, she would have quite a useful amount of money.

She carefully locked away all her possessions, but kept out a cheque from George Osborne for gambling debts. This made her think of Mrs Osborne. 'I'll get the cheque cashed,' she said to herself, 'and pay a visit afterwards to poor little Emmy.'

✿

Joseph Sedley, of course, was not a soldier and had no goodbyes to say. However, he was disturbed from his sleep before daybreak by Captain Dobbin, who insisted on shaking hands with him.

'I didn't want to go without saying goodbye,' he said.

'Very kind of you,' said Jos, yawning, and rubbing his eyes.

'Some of us – well, some of us may not come back again – and – and I want to be sure that you'll all be all right.'

Jos and the Osbornes shared a sitting-room in their hotel apartment, and while Dobbin was speaking, he kept walking up and down, glancing through the open door of Jos's bedroom into the sitting-room, hoping desperately for a last sight of Amelia.

Jos stared at his visitor as he marched up and down. 'What can I do for you, Dobbin?' he said at last, rather crossly.

'I'll tell you what you can do,' Dobbin said. 'George and I may never come back. You are not to move from this town until you know what has happened. You are to watch over your sister, and comfort her, and make sure that no harm comes to her. Remember, if anything happens to George, she has no one but you. You must promise me that you will never leave her.'

'Of course I'll take care of my sister,' answered Jos.

'And you must see that she gets safely out of Brussels and back to England in the event of a defeat.'

'Defeat! Don't try and frighten *me*,' cried our hero, in his bed.

At that moment Dobbin had the opportunity he wanted so much – to see Amelia's face again. But what a face – so white, so wild, so despairing! Shocked, Dobbin stood and watched her, torn with pity for such helpless, speechless misery.

Wrapped in a white morning dress and with her hair hanging loose, Amelia was trying to help George as he did his packing. At last, however, George took her hand and led her back into the bedroom. He came out alone, and hurried away.

'Thank Heaven that's over,' he thought, running downstairs to join the regiment, who were gathering in the street below.

The sun was just rising as the soldiers marched away. It was a brave sight, with the band playing, and the bright flags flying, and George marching proudly at the head of his company. He looked up, and smiled at Amelia, and passed on; and even the sound of the music died away.

All day Brussels waited for news of the battle. Stories flew around the city – Napoleon's army was advancing, the Duke of Wellington was wounded, the British had suffered great losses. Shops closed, and soon carriages began to leave the city.

Jos, who had felt quite brave and confident in the morning, now began to fear the worst. He was just putting on his coat to go out for the latest news on the street, when Rebecca arrived to visit Amelia. Her smiling face, refreshed by her quiet sleep, was pleasant to see in a town where everyone else looked anxious.

'Are you leaving us to join the army, Mr Joseph?' she said, looking at his coat, which was cut in a military style. 'How brave you are! But then who will be left to protect us poor women? Oh, please don't leave us, Mr Joseph!'

What Rebecca really meant was, 'Sir, you have a comfortable carriage, and if the army is defeated and we have to leave Brussels, I would like a seat in it.'

Jos had been deeply offended by Rebecca's treatment of him in Brussels. She had paid little attention to him, and had not invited him to her parties. 'She only wants me when there is no one else,' he thought. But a vain man is always pleased to be called brave, and wiser men than Jos Sedley have been fooled by women. A few soft words, some admiring glances from those sparkling green eyes, and it was not long before Jos's heart was beating fast, and his doubts and suspicions were all forgotten.

Presently, Rebecca left him, confident of her place in his carriage, and went to tap gently at the door of his sister's room.

Her appearance struck Amelia with terror. It brought her back to the real world, and reminded her of the jealous misery that had been forgotten in the pain of parting from her adored husband. And when Rebecca came forward to kiss her, Amelia, her pale face suddenly red with anger, returned Rebecca's look with a steadiness that rather surprised her visitor.

'Dearest Amelia, you are not well.' Rebecca put out her hand to take Amelia's. 'I could not rest until I knew how you were.'

Amelia did not take the offered hand. 'Why are *you* here, Rebecca?' she said, looking at her with her large eyes.

This worried Rebecca. 'She must have seen him give me the letter at the ball,' she thought. 'Don't be upset, dear Amelia,' she said. 'I only came to see if I could – if you were well.'

'Are you well?' said Amelia. 'I'm sure you are. You don't love your husband. You would not be here if you did. Tell me, Rebecca, was I ever unkind to you?'

'Indeed, Amelia, no,' Rebecca said, looking away from her.

'When you were poor, I was your friend. George loved me. He gave up his fortune and his family to marry me, to make me happy. Why did you come between us? His love was everything to me. You knew it, and wanted to steal it from me. You are a wicked woman, Rebecca – a false friend and a false wife!'

49

'Amelia, I swear that I have done my husband no wrong.'

'Have you done *me* no wrong, Rebecca? You did not succeed, but you tried.'

She knows nothing, Rebecca thought.

'He came back to me. Your tricks and lies could not keep him for long. But what have I done to you? Why did you try to take him from me?' Amelia's voice became wilder. 'And now he's gone. But he will come back. He promised me to come back.'

'He will come back, my dear,' said Rebecca, gently.

Amelia walked to a chair and knelt beside it. 'He was here,' she said. 'He sat here, in this chair.' She seemed to have forgotten Rebecca's presence, and began to stroke the arm of the chair.

Rebecca turned and left the room silently. 'How is she?' asked Jos, who was still sitting in the sitting-room.

'There should be somebody with her,' said Rebecca. 'I think she is very unwell.' And she went away, with a very serious face.

She did, in fact, like Amelia, and felt some pity for her. She thought of the little note locked away in her writing-desk. 'Poor thing! That note would destroy her. Why does she break her heart for a man who is stupid – and who does not care for her?'

By late afternoon the sound of gunfire could be heard in the city, and few people had much sleep that night. The next day brought wounded soldiers returning from the battlefield, with reports of regiments destroyed, and Napoleon closing in on Brussels.

Like many others, Joseph Sedley was now desperate to leave, but his servant told him there were no horses to hire or to buy anywhere in the city. Wild with terror, Jos shaved off his moustache, in case the enemy thought he was a soldier, and set out into the city to search for horses himself.

As he passed Rebecca's hotel, he caught sight of her and hurried over. By now, the two horses which Rawdon had left behind were extremely valuable, and one look at Jos's fat, frightened face told Rebecca that she had found a buyer who would pay whatever price she asked.

'What! Are you leaving, Mr Sedley?' she said, with a laugh. 'And Amelia? Who is to protect your poor little sister?'

'There's a seat for her in my carriage,' gasped Jos. 'And for you, dear Mrs Crawley, if only I can find horses!'

'I have two to sell,' said Becky. 'But they're not carriage horses. You'll have to ride them.'

Jos nearly wept for joy. The business was soon done, and Jos was obliged to part with an enormous amount of money.

That night there was more encouraging news of the battle, but by Sunday morning the guns of Waterloo began to roar. When Jos heard that dreadful sound, he could bear it no longer.

'You must come with me, Emmy!' he cried, rushing into her room. 'I have bought a horse for you. You must come!'

'Without my husband, Joseph?' Amelia said, with a look of wonder. But Jos's patience was at an end.

'Goodbye, then,' he shouted angrily, banging the door shut as he left. And he got on his horse, and with his servant he rode away out of Brussels, leaving his sister behind him.

All that day, from morning until past sunset, the guns roared, and the women prayed for their husbands and lovers. On a hill on the battlefield the lines of English foot-soldiers stood firm against the furious attacks of the French, who were forced to fall back again and again. In the evening, the French made a final big attack. Then at last the English roared down from the hill-top which they had held all day, and the enemy turned and ran.

Joseph rode away out of Brussels, leaving his sister behind him.

In Brussels the guns could be heard no more. Darkness came down on the battlefield and on the city; and Amelia was praying for George, who was lying on his face, dead, with a bullet through his heart.

6

Mothers, sons, and other relations

Captain Rawdon Crawley, although a big man and so an easy mark for a shot, returned safe and well from the battle of Waterloo. Indeed, his bravery on the battlefield was so great that it brought him promotion to Colonel Crawley.

Becky rejoined her husband at Cambray, a town some miles north of Paris. When she left Brussels, careful little woman that she was, she travelled with all her valuables sewn into her clothes. On meeting Rawdon, she unsewed herself and brought out all the jewellery, cheques, and bank-notes hidden in her long skirts.

Rawdon roared with delighted laughter. 'This is better than a play at the theatre!' he said.

'And the best joke of all is this,' said Becky, holding up a particularly thick bunch of bank-notes.

Rawdon's eyes opened wide. 'Where did you get all that?' he asked.

'By selling your horses to Joseph Sedley. You should have seen him! He was in such a dreadful hurry to run away from Napoleon that he didn't care what he paid.'

'Becky, you're a wonder,' said her husband.

The army marched to Paris, and Becky and Rawdon passed the winter of 1815 there, living in fine style. In fact, the money that poor Jos Sedley had paid for those horses was enough to support the Crawleys for at least a year.

They continued, of course, to have high hopes of Miss Matilda Crawley, and indeed it was well known in Paris that Colonel Rawdon and his so charming wife expected to inherit a large fortune from the gentleman's aunt.

The gentleman's aunt, however, took a different view of the matter. Miss Briggs, her faithful companion, had been deeply impressed by Colonel Rawdon's bravery at Waterloo.

'The Colonel has brought fame to the name of Crawley,' she said. 'Don't you feel a little sympathy for your brave nephew?'

'Briggs, you're a fool,' said Miss Crawley. 'The Colonel has brought *shame* to the name of Crawley. He could have married into a good family – but no, he married a drawing-teacher's daughter, a nobody. She was just what you are, Briggs, only younger and a great deal prettier and cleverer. Rawdon would have had my money one day. But not now. Oh no!'

The truth was that Miss Crawley had a new favourite now, her dear niece-to-be, Lady Jane. Mr Pitt Crawley, Rawdon's older brother, had for some time been visiting his aunt quite frequently. He introduced her to his bride-to-be, Lady Jane, a pleasant, kindly young woman, who was from a grand and well-connected family. Miss Crawley approved of the family, approved of Lady Jane, and approved of the marriage.

She received many amusing letters from Rawdon in Paris (written, of course, by Becky), but however amusing the letters were, they did not soften her heart. Moreover, she heard from an old friend in Paris that Becky was shamelessly using Miss Crawley's name to gain acceptance in Parisian society. This made Miss Crawley wild with anger.

And then, in the spring of 1816, Miss Briggs read out to her this announcement in the London newspaper:

BIRTHS

To Colonel and Mrs Rawdon Crawley, a son

Miss Crawley's fury with Rawdon rose to new heights, and she sent for Pitt Crawley.

'You must marry Lady Jane at once,' she said. 'I will give you and my dear niece a thousand pounds a year during my lifetime, and when I die, the two of you will inherit everything.'

With such encouragement the marriage was soon completed, and the happy couple went to live with their affectionate aunt.

Unaware of the end of their financial hopes, Rawdon and Becky continued to live an easy, pleasant life in Paris. Their little son, also called Rawdon, spent the first eighteen months of his life with a nurse in a village, thus enabling his mother to continue with her brilliant social life in the city. The Colonel, however, was a fond father, often riding out to visit little Rawdon.

As time went on, Becky saw that their easy, pleasant life could not continue. Their money was nearly all gone, they were deeply in debt, and although Rawdon's great skill at billiards and cards gave him many gambling successes, it was not a reliable income. Indeed, many young officers now left Mrs Crawley's parties with sad faces, having lost rather too much money at her card-tables. Warnings were whispered to the inexperienced, and her house began to have an unfortunate reputation.

'We must think about the future,' Becky said to Rawdon. 'Gambling is good to help your income, my dear, but not as an income itself. One day people may grow tired of gambling, and then where will we be?'

'That's true,' said Rawdon gloomily. 'Some of the fellows I play with are not so keen on playing as they used to be.'

'You must leave the army, and we must go back to England,' Becky said. 'We must find you a government appointment in London, or perhaps a position as a Governor abroad.'

At this point news reached Paris of Miss Crawley's death, delighting the many people to whom the Crawleys owed money. Naturally, the Crawleys hurried back to London to collect the enormous inheritance that the Colonel was expecting. They would soon return to Paris, Mrs Crawley told everyone, to pay all their bills, and to rent a grander house. As evidence of this intention, they left behind several boxes of possessions – which were later opened and found to be full of worthless rubbish.

No such inheritance, of course, was waiting for the Crawleys in London, but they rented a charming little house in Curzon Street and began a new life. Their unfortunate landlord received no rent, their servants no wages, and the suppliers of food and wine and dresses and carriages were not paid either. But the Crawleys lived well, and once again their debts grew and grew.

Becky's social success was not the same in London, however. The grand English ladies who had been pleased to know her in Paris now turned cold, unsmiling faces away when they saw her.

This made Rawdon furious. 'I'll *make* these women respect you,' he said. 'I'll fight their husbands, their brothers, and – and shoot the lot of them!'

'You can't shoot me into society, my dear,' said Becky, smiling. 'Remember that I was only a governess before, and you, you poor silly boy, have the worst reputation for debt, and gambling, and all sorts of wickedness.'

'What are we to do then? We'll be ruined,' said Rawdon.

'Nonsense! While there is life there is hope, my dear, and I intend to make a man of you yet. Who sold your horses for you in Brussels? Who stopped you shouting the news all round Paris that your aunt had left everything to Pitt and Lady Jane?'

'That damned brother of mine!' said Rawdon. 'Why should that pale-faced idiot and his boring little wife get everything, eh?'

'Losing your temper again won't get us your aunt's money,' said his wife calmly. 'We need to be friends with your brother's family, and this is what you must do. You must write a nice letter to Pitt. You will congratulate him on his good fortune. You will be full of affection for your brother, respect for his wife, and kindness for their children. And you will beg their friendship for us and our little boy. Come – sit down and write it now.'

*

Colonel Rawdon Crawley had survived the battle of Waterloo, and so had William Dobbin, now promoted from Captain to Major. But many other officers had not survived, and when the news of George Osborne's death was brought to Amelia, it nearly killed her. For weeks she lay in a darkened room while doctors feared for her life. Eventually, she left her bed, and began living again. But sorrow had changed her. Her face was white and thin, her eyes empty of expression, and she accepted friendship and kindness without complaint, and without interest.

Throughout this time, Dobbin was never far away from her, and always accompanied her when she went for a drive. One day he was riding as usual by the side of her carriage when he thought he saw George's father in a carriage coming towards them.

It was indeed Mr Osborne. His son's death had been a terrible shock to him, and he had never spoken his name, not even when he received George's last letter, written the night before the battle. The poor boy wrote that he wished to say goodbye to his father and, if anything should happen to him, he begged his father to take care of his wife, and perhaps, his child. A few months later, Mr Osborne announced that he was going abroad, and his daughters had little doubt that he would go to Brussels.

He had visited his son's grave, seen the battlefield where his son died, and was returning to his hotel when he passed Amelia's carriage. She was so changed that he did not recognize her until he saw Dobbin at her side. For a second he stared at her, then he called to his servant to drive on.

But Dobbin rode after him. Amelia, poor girl, had neither recognized her father-in-law, nor noticed that Dobbin had gone.

'Mr Osborne, Mr Osborne!' cried Dobbin, riding up beside him and holding out his hand. Osborne made no move to take it, and shouted again to his servant to drive on.

Dobbin laid his hand on the side of the carriage. 'I will see you, sir,' he said. 'I have a message for you.'

'From that woman?' said Osborne fiercely.

'No,' replied Dobbin. 'From your son.'

Mr Osborne fell back in his carriage, but said nothing. Dobbin rode behind him and then followed him into his hotel.

'I am here as George's closest friend,' Dobbin began when they were face to face. 'He left hardly any money when he died. Are you aware how little his widow has to live on?'

'I don't know his widow, sir,' said Osborne. 'Let her go back to her father.'

'Do you know, sir, Mrs Osborne's condition?' Dobbin went on. 'She has been very ill. In fact, she may die. There is just one thing which may save her. She will soon be a mother. Will you not forgive the child for poor George's sake?'

Osborne stared at Dobbin angrily. 'My son was a disobedient fool, and he brought this on himself. I am a man of my word. I swore I would never speak to that woman, nor recognize her as my son's wife, and that is what you may tell her.'

But Major Dobbin did not tell Amelia about his meeting with Mr Osborne. She would not have cared, for her thoughts were only for her dead husband. But the day came when the poor widowed girl held a child in her arms, a child with the eyes of George who was gone – a beautiful little boy. How she laughed and wept over this baby! And what joy it gave her friends to see her eyes once again shining with love.

Our friend Dobbin was one of them. It was he who brought her back to England, and home to her parents. He visited them every day, and brought gifts for the child, and sometimes he was allowed to hold the baby. Amelia wrapped her child in love, and Dobbin could see that there was no place for him in her heart. He bore this knowledge gently, without complaining.

One day he arrived carrying toys for little Georgy – a wooden horse, a trumpet, and all kinds of warlike toys. The landlord's little daughter, who was often with Amelia and was one of the few people allowed to play with the baby, laughed, as Georgy was only six months old, much too young for such toys.

The child was asleep. 'Hush!' said Amelia as Dobbin came in.

'I have come to say goodbye, Amelia,' he said quietly.

'Goodbye? Where are you going?' she said, with a smile.

'To India, with the regiment,' he said. 'You will write to me, won't you? I'll be away a long time.'

'I'll write to you about Georgy,' she said. 'Dear William, you have been so kind to us. Look at him. Isn't he wonderful?'

Amelia looked up at Dobbin, her face bright with motherly pride, and he saw that his leaving meant nothing to her. For a moment he could not speak; then, 'Goodbye,' he said.

'Goodbye,' said Amelia, and held up her face and kissed him.

'Hush! Don't wake Georgy!' she added, as Dobbin went to the door with heavy steps. She did not hear his carriage drive away; she was looking at the child, who was laughing in his sleep.

One day Major Dobbin arrived carrying toys for little Georgy.

Reunions, quarrels, & other family business

Pitt Crawley was astonished to receive such a pleasant letter from his brother Rawdon. His wife Lady Jane, a gentle, kindly woman, was delighted, and expected that Pitt would immediately divide his aunt's inheritance into two equal parts and send one to his brother.

Pitt did not feel the need to send a cheque to Rawdon for thirty thousand pounds, but he did write back in a friendly manner, promising to help his brother and his family if he could.

The brothers did not meet for some time, however. Since the death of Miss Crawley, Pitt and Lady Jane had been living down at Queen's Crawley, where Becky had gone as governess years before. Her former employer, Sir Pitt Crawley, was still alive, but even more disagreeable than he used to be, and when he finally died a few years later, none of his family felt any great sorrow.

In fact, when the black-edged invitation to the funeral arrived in Curzon Street, the reactions were very far from sorrowful.

Rawdon carried the letter to Becky in her bedroom – with her cup of chocolate, which he always took to her every morning.

'We don't have to go, do we, Becky?' he said. 'Pitt bores me to death, and a carriage there and back will cost too much.'

'Of course we're going, you silly man!' cried Becky, jumping up in delight. 'Your brother is now *Sir* Pitt, and a Member of Parliament. I want Lady Jane to present me at court next year, and I want Sir Pitt to get you a position of some importance – the Governor of the West Indies, or something like that. We must order our black clothes for the funeral at once.'

'Little Rawdy comes too, of course,' said her husband.

'Of course not! Why pay for a third seat in the carriage?'

It was a great moment when the two Crawley brothers met again at last. The new Sir Pitt shook his brother warmly by the hand, while Lady Jane took both Becky's hands, and kissed her.

This mark of kindness brought tears to Becky's eyes, which was a rare event. When Lady Jane took Becky to her room, Becky at once began work on earning her sister-in-law's approval.

'What I should like to do first,' Becky said, in a soft little voice, 'is to see your dear little children.'

This request pleased Lady Jane very much. She led Becky away to meet her daughter and son, aged four and two, and in no time at all, she and Becky were close and affectionate friends.

'You must be so sad,' Lady Jane said sympathetically, 'to have left your little boy in London.'

'Dear, dear Rawdy!' sighed Becky. 'I miss him so much.'

It was fortunate that her husband did not hear this remark as it would have surprised him greatly. He was very fond of his son. He saw Rawdy every day at home, bought him presents and toys, played with him whenever he could. His mother took no notice of the boy at all. When he cried at night, it was a servant who came and took him to her room to comfort him.

Rawdon and Becky spent several days at Queen's Crawley, and it was time well spent. Lady Jane thought Becky was delightful, and Sir Pitt also approved of her. She had shown interest in his ambitions for government, and made admiring comments on his political ideas, which he had found very agreeable.

'I did not like the marriage at the time,' he told his wife, 'but it has improved Rawdon very much.'

Rawdon was almost sorry to leave, but Becky was glad to escape from playing the part of a dutiful sister-in-law – listening with interest to dull conversations, inspecting the fruit garden, visiting sick villagers with soup and encouragement.

'It isn't difficult to be a country gentleman's wife,' she said to Rawdon in the carriage returning to London. 'I think I could be a good woman if I had five thousand a year.'

'Mm,' said Rawdon. 'I wish you'd got some money out of Pitt, though. I'd like to pay the landlord some of the rent we owe. It isn't right, you know, that his family should starve because of us.'

'Pitt gave me this for Rawdy,' Becky said. It was a cheque for a small amount. 'Give it to the landlord. We've been invited to Queen's Crawley for Christmas – perhaps Pitt will do something for you then. Or next year, when they come to London. Until then we must manage on your winnings at cards. And perhaps Lord Steyne will hear of a position for you.'

This Lord Steyne was one of Becky's admirers in London. High-society women still ignored her, but the men crowded to Mrs Crawley's little house, where the suppers were excellent, and the conversation brilliant. And where many of them, of course, lost money at the card-tables to Colonel Crawley.

Not Lord Steyne, however, who was no fool. He was a short, ugly man, disliked by many for his cruel tongue and his evil reputation. But he was extremely wealthy, belonged to one of the grandest families in England, and dined with the Prince of Wales. It comforted the poor landlord to see Lord Steyne's carriage outside the Crawleys' door. With such rich friends, he thought, they were sure to pay his rent one day . . .

Becky amused Lord Steyne. He admired her charm and her intelligence and her cunning, which he saw was equal to his own, and her artful lies gave him much entertainment. He laughed a great deal at Becky's account of her time at Queen's Crawley.

'I should like to see you visiting the sick,' he said, 'and being polite to those dull relations of your husband's.'

'They are very good people,' said Becky sternly. 'You should not laugh at them.'

Lord Steyne laughed again. 'And you, my pretty lady, were bored to tears by them all. Come now, admit it, Mrs Crawley!'

Becky gave a wicked little smile, but would admit nothing, and after taking some tea, Lord Steyne went away. On the way out he met Rawdon, and greeted him in his usual manner.

'How is Mrs Crawley's husband?' he would say, and indeed, in London that is what Rawdon had become. He was Colonel Crawley no more; he was Mrs Crawley's husband.

Rawdon was still very fond of his wife. He admired her brilliance and her clever conversation, and obeyed her orders without question. But he had few interests apart from gambling and horses, and was glad whenever Becky released him from his social duties and sent him off to dine with his friends.

'Some gentlemen are coming tonight who would bore you,' she would say. 'I only invite them because they have influence and can help you. And now I have a companion, there's no need for you to be here.'

The companion was Miss Briggs, who had been companion to Rawdon's aunt until that lady died. Becky, hearing that Miss Briggs had inherited some money from Miss Crawley, had invited her to Curzon Street as her companion. Miss Briggs's friends warned her against the Crawleys, but Miss Briggs went to live with Mrs Rawdon the next week, and had lent Rawdon Crawley six hundred pounds before six months were over.

Her presence in the house made it possible for Becky to receive gentleman visitors when her husband was not at home, and although Lord Steyne often growled at her 'watch-dog', as he called Miss Briggs, Becky only laughed.

Miss Briggs also helped to look after little Rawdon. He was now seven years old, a fine, strong boy, with a gentle nature, fond of everyone who was good to him, especially Miss Briggs and his father. He no longer thought of his mother in that way.

For two years she had hardly spoken to him. She disliked him, and he bored her. One day, attracted by the sound of his mother's voice singing, he came quietly downstairs. The drawing-room door opened suddenly and revealed the boy standing there, listening in delight to the music.

His mother came out and struck him violently on the ear. He heard a laugh from Lord Steyne inside the room (who was amused by this display of Becky's bad temper), and he ran away, down to his friends the servants in the kitchen.

'It isn't because it hurts,' he said, crying bitterly, 'but why can't I listen to her singing? She sings to that bald-headed man with the big teeth. Why doesn't she sing to me?'

From that day Becky hated her son. And the boy began to feel fear and doubt. He knew that this man was his enemy. Whenever they met, Lord Steyne would make some nasty remark, and in return, the child would stare hard at him and put his hands up as though to fight him.

When Christmas came and the visit to Queen's Crawley, Becky wanted to leave the child behind, but Lady Jane insisted that he came too. Rawdon complained at Becky's neglect of their son.

'He's the finest boy in England,' he said, 'but you don't seem to love him as much as you do your little dog. He won't bother you much. He'll be with the other children all the time, and on the journey he can ride outside on the coach with me.'

'You only sit outside on the coach so you can smoke those awful cigars,' said Becky.

'You always used to like the smell of cigars,' Rawdon said.

His wife laughed. 'That was before we were married,' she said.

So little Rawdon accompanied them to Queen's Crawley, and he loved every minute. When they arrived, Sir Pitt and Lady Jane and their children were there to welcome them in the hall, and the little girl, Matilda, shyly kissed Rawdy on the cheek.

The children were soon firm friends, with Rawdy, who was the oldest, the leader in all their games. He also loved going with his father to the stables, or helping in the hunt for rats in the farm buildings. But best of all, he loved his Aunt Jane, who was so kind to him. He even allowed her to kiss him sometimes. In the evenings, after dinner, when the ladies went to the drawing-room and left the gentlemen to drink their wine, he always preferred to sit near his Aunt Jane, rather than his mother.

One evening when there were guests, Becky, having noticed that Lady Jane and the other ladies were in the habit of kissing their children, called her son over to her and kissed him.

He looked her full in the face after the kiss, trembling and turning very red. 'You never kiss me at home, mama,' he said.

An embarrassed silence fell in the room, and there was a rather unpleasant look in Becky's eyes.

After that day Lady Jane and Becky were never quite so friendly. There was a coolness in the air, and Lady Jane began to feel that her husband was paying Becky too much attention.

They spent hours in his study, discussing his political ambitions and plans – subjects that Sir Pitt never mentioned to his wife.

Rawdon had become fond of his sister-in-law because she was so kind to his son, and when the holiday was over, both he and

Sir Pitt and Lady Jane and their children were there to welcome them.

his son were sad to leave. The ladies, however, said goodbye to each other with less sadness. Becky was keen to return to the bright lights of London. She was bored with the country and bored with the sweet and gentle Lady Jane, though of course she was careful not to reveal this, as she needed Lady Jane to present her at court. She was determined to climb the social ladder as high as she could, determined to show those proud, stiff-necked society women that she, Rebecca Sharp, daughter of a drawing- teacher, could outshine them all in social brilliance.

While Becky was busily making new friends and new enemies, her former friend Amelia found her social circle was shrinking. Dobbin had gone to India, and her brother Joseph had returned to his job there soon after the battle of Waterloo. Perhaps he had been afraid that his terrified flight from Brussels might be talked about and laughed at. However, he made an allowance to his parents of a hundred and twenty pounds a year, paid monthly through his London agent.

Mr Sedley borrowed money to try to recover his lost fortune, but his attempts to start new businesses became more and more foolish, and he lost the money he had borrowed. Amelia had a small widow's pension, and with Joseph's money, the little family had just enough to live on.

Amelia's whole life was centred on her son Georgy. She was extremely possessive about him, and wanted to do everything for him herself. Once, when Georgy was still a baby, she came into her room and found her mother giving the child a spoonful of Daffy's Special Baby Medicine.

Amelia seized the baby out of her mother's arms, then grabbed the bottle of medicine and sent it crashing into the fireplace.

'I will *not* have my baby poisoned, mama!' she cried.

'Poisoned, Amelia?' said the old lady. 'What are you saying?'

'Georgy shall not have any medicine unless the doctor approves of it. And he told me that Daffy's was poison.'

'Very good; you think I'm a murderess,' said Mrs Sedley. 'I have met with misfortunes; I have sunk low in life; but I did not know I was a murderess before, and thank you for the *news*.'

'Oh, mama,' said the poor girl, 'I didn't mean—'

'Oh no, my love, – only that I was a murderess. Though I didn't poison *you* when you were a child. A murderess, indeed! May God forgive you, you wicked, ungrateful girl!'

After this, there was a coolness between mother and daughter that never really went away. Mrs Sedley had little to do with her grandson and was frequently critical of her daughter.

Georgy grew up to look very like his father, and Amelia spoke to him constantly of her love for her dead husband, whose picture hung on the wall above her bed, and was cleaned daily.

Amelia was not without admirers in her little social circle. She was not brilliant, nor clever, nor wise, nor very pretty, but men were always charmed by her. Perhaps it was her weakness and her sweet nature that made men want to protect her. But it was certain that young Mr Linton, the doctor's assistant, was her willing slave. He sat up through the night with Georgy during his childhood illnesses, and would call in at any time, without a fee, if Mrs Osborne was at all worried about her darling boy.

Amelia kept her promise to Dobbin and wrote to him two or three times a year – letters all about little Georgy. Dobbin was delighted to receive these letters, and always replied. He sent many gifts too – beautiful Indian shawls for Amelia and her mother, wonderful carved wooden animals for Georgy.

'It's quite obvious,' Mrs Sedley remarked to the landlady, 'that Major Dobbin is in love with her, but whenever I mention the fact, she begins to cry, and goes and sits upstairs with her little picture of George. I'm sick of that picture. I wish we'd never seen those horrid, proud Osbornes.'

Georgy grew up surrounded by love, ruling the little world around him, including his gentle mother, whom he loved with a passionate affection. Everyone was amazed at how like his father he was – the same face, the same hair, even the same pride.

Dobbin's letters continued to take a close interest in Georgy, asking about his reading and writing, wanting to know if he was going to school, and offering to help with the fees.

Sometimes his sister, Miss Dobbin (no doubt on her brother's instructions), came to visit Amelia and Georgy; and sometimes she begged that the boy might spend a day with her at home. Unwillingly, Amelia agreed to this, but Georgy loved his days at Miss Dobbin's home, where there was a wonderful garden to play in, and wonderful fruit to eat from the hot-houses.

One day Miss Dobbin arrived with some *very* interesting news about her brother William that she was *sure* would delight Amelia.

'Is he coming home?' Amelia asked, looking pleased.

'Oh, no,' his sister replied. 'Not at all. But I have very good reason to believe that dear William is about to be married – to a most lovely girl, everybody says.'

'Oh!' said Amelia. She was very, *very* happy indeed. But her eyes seemed a little damp, and she was strangely silent for the rest of the day – though she was very happy indeed at the news.

8

The rise and fall of our heroines' fortunes

Mrs Rawdon Crawley knew that to gain acceptance into the highest society, she must be presented to the King at court. After she had made her curtsy to the highest person in the land, the noble families of England would be obliged, however unwillingly, to recognize her.

Her sister-in-law, Lady Jane, being from a noble family, was the ideal person to present Becky at court, so Becky made herself very agreeable to Sir Pitt when he was in London. She helped him write his political speeches, and discussed political events with him. She introduced him to important gentlemen at her parties, and he was deeply impressed by Becky's friendly relationship with the wealthy Lord Steyne. He had no idea that behind his back Becky made fun of him to the great Lord.

While his house in Great Gaunt Street was being made ready for his family, Sir Pitt stayed in Curzon Street, where Becky daily fussed over his comfort. One evening she even cooked a little supper for him with her own hands.

'It is an excellent meal, my dear Rebecca,' said Sir Pitt. 'But everything you do, you do well.'

'A poor man's wife,' Becky replied cheerfully, 'must make herself useful, you know.'

'You could be the wife of a king, with all your skills,' Sir Pitt said. He thought to himself how Rawdon was a foolish, dull fellow, who didn't appreciate his brilliant wife; and how pretty Becky looked, sitting opposite him at the table.

And later, sitting by the fire, Becky let him talk, listening to him with kindly interest and sewing a shirt for her dear little son. Whenever she wished to appear a model of wifely goodness, this little shirt was brought out of her sewing-box. It was too small for Rawdy long before it was finished.

When the house in Great Gaunt Street was ready and Lady Jane had moved in, Becky would call on her from time to time, but in general the two women saw little of each other. Sir Pitt, however, found time to see his sister-in-law daily, and was a regular guest at her evening parties.

In the middle of these fine parties and brilliant people, Colonel Rawdon found himself more isolated every day. He was rarely required for social duties these days, and would often walk round to Gaunt Street with young Rawdy, and sit with Lady Jane and the children. He was glad to be given small jobs to do – taking messages, helping with the children's dinner. The brave and daring young soldier of ten years before had become a dull, lazy, obedient, middle-aged gentleman.

And poor Lady Jane knew that her husband had become a victim of Becky's charm, although when they met, she and Mrs Rawdon still behaved as though they were the best of friends.

At last Becky's kindness and attention to the head of her husband's family were given their due reward, and the great day came when Sir Pitt's carriage arrived in Curzon Street to take Mrs Rawdon Crawley and her husband to meet the King.

Becky's dress that day put the dresses of all other women in the shade, as even Lady Jane was forced to admit.

And the diamonds . . . 'Where the devil did you get the diamonds, Becky?' said her husband, admiring the jewels which sparkled on her arms and neck with great brilliance.

Becky blushed a little, and looked at him hard. Pitt Crawley blushed too, and looked uneasy. He had given her a little bracelet himself – but had failed to mention this fact to his wife.

Becky smiled at Rawdon. 'Guess!' she said. 'Where do you think I got them, you silly man? I hired them, of course.'

Becky's diamonds, however, never returned to any hire-shop. They were later locked away in a secret little desk that she had, and Rawdon knew nothing about the diamonds which shone on his wife's neck that day.

But Lord Steyne knew where the jewels came from, and who paid for them. As he bowed over Becky's hand in the royal rooms that day, he gave her a knowing smile, which was returned. And many people there noted the particular attention that the great Lord Steyne paid to the Colonel's little wife.

And so began Becky's victory over her enemies. How angrily did those grand ladies now send their cards of invitation to Mrs Rawdon Crawley! How they smiled at her, tight-lipped and with icy stares! How Becky's eyes sparkled with delight at their silent and terrible fury! And the more the ladies hated her, the more the gentlemen were devoted in their admiration. Hungarian princes sighed over her little hand, government ministers begged her to sing to them at evening parties, handsome young men competed with each other to fetch her shawl, to hold her carriage door, to write poems in praise of her bright eyes.

Lord Steyne was amused by Becky's victorious social progress. 'It won't last,' he told her. 'You can't compete with them for long, you silly little fool. You have no money.'

Becky turned her big green eyes on him and sighed. 'You must get my husband a position,' she said, 'as soon as possible.'

'All women are the same,' said the noble Lord. 'Wanting this, demanding that. None of it is worth having.'

Miss Briggs, seated at the work-table at the back of the room, looked up nervously at the sound of his fierce voice. Lord Steyne saw her looking, and turned angrily to Becky.

'Why don't you get rid of your watch-dog?' he growled.

Becky laughed, but a little later suggested to Miss Briggs that she took Rawdy out for a walk in the park.

'I can't send her away,' Becky said sadly, when she had gone.

'You owe her her wages, I suppose?' said Lord Steyne.

'Yes, and worse than that,' said Becky. 'I have ruined her. I have borrowed all her savings, and can't pay a penny back. My husband would kill me if he knew.'

There was a brief silence. 'Damned fool!' said the Lord. 'How much is it?'

Becky thought about the size of Lord Steyne's fortune, and mentioned an amount twice the size of the debt to Miss Briggs. Lord Steyne swore again, at which Becky held her head down and began to cry bitterly. Lord Steyne then took his hat and left.

That night Becky received a note with Lord Steyne's signature, and an instruction to his bankers. In the morning she hurried to the bank. How will you take the money, madam? A hundred and fifty pounds in small notes, and the rest in one note.

On the way home she stopped to buy a handsome black silk dress for Miss Briggs. She called into the landlord's house and gave him fifty pounds on account, and did the same at the stables where she hired her carriages. The one note that the bank had given her she locked away in her secret little desk.

Lord Steyne continued to be generous to the Crawley family. He pointed out to the parents that it was time young Rawdy was sent away to a good school, and when the father said he could not pay the fees, Lord Steyne offered to take care of the matter. Rawdon agreed to the plan for his son's sake, but he missed the boy greatly, and was sad and lonely when he had gone.

Becky hardly noticed that her son had gone. Nor did she notice her husband's unhappiness. She was too busy thinking about her position, her pleasures, her advancement in society.

Having got rid of the child, Lord Steyne suggested before long that there was no further need for Miss Briggs in the Crawley household. He found out from the lady herself how Becky had deceived him about the money, and this amused him greatly.

'What a clever little devil she is!' he thought. 'I'm a fool compared to her. She's the best liar I have ever met!'

He arranged a pleasant, well-paid job for Miss Briggs in one of his country houses. Miss Briggs was delighted with the plan, and Rawdon was glad that Miss Briggs would at last receive some wages, even if the debt to her was still unpaid. But he was uneasy in his mind. His brother shared his unease.

'Rebecca should not receive guests without a companion,' Sir Pitt said. 'You must be with her, Rawdon, at all times.'

In fact, Sir Pitt was so alarmed that he went to see Becky and came close to a quarrel with his once admired sister-in-law.

'People are talking about you,' he said. 'These wild young men of fashion who visit you, the fact that Lord Steyne's carriage is always at your door – it's not only *your* reputation that suffers, but that of the whole Crawley family. I am the head of the family and I beg you, I command you, to be more careful.'

Tears, smiles, excuses – nothing would calm Sir Pitt, and

Becky promised everything Pitt wanted; but Lord Steyne came to her house as often as ever, and Sir Pitt's anger increased.

Rawdon, aware of his brother's anger, became more watchful. He stopped gambling and stayed at home. He went with Becky to all her parties. Whenever Lord Steyne visited, he was sure to find the Colonel there.

The great and noble Lord Steyne bowed low before Becky.

Becky was charmed by Rawdon's attention. 'How much nicer it is to have you by my side than foolish old Briggs!' she said. 'How happy we would be, if we only had money.'

It was like the early days of their marriage over again, and Rawdon wondered why he had ever had suspicions. She was fond of him; she always had been. As for her shining in society, it was no fault of hers; she was made to shine. Was there any woman who could talk, or sing, or do anything like her?

At one grand party at Lord Steyne's house, when a very Royal person was present, Rawdon was reminded yet again of his wife's social success. It was a night when charades were played, and Becky acted the part of Clytemnestra, a Greek queen of long ago who murdered her husband. The style and brilliance of her acting delighted the guests. The company roared their admiration, the Royal person said she was perfection itself, and the great and noble Lord Steyne bowed low before her.

Rawdon Crawley was frightened by Becky's success. It seemed to separate his wife from him further than ever. He thought, with a feeling very like pain, how much above him she was. At the end of the evening he put his wife into the carriage, and decided to go home himself on foot, enjoying a cigar as he walked.

He did not notice the men following him until one of them, touching him on the shoulder, said,

'Excuse me, Colonel, I wish to speak to you.'

Rawdon looked round.

'There's three of us. No use running,' the man said.

Rawdon threw away his cigar. He knew exactly what was happening to him, because it had happened to him before. He was being arrested for debt.

In the quiet suburb of London where the Sedleys lived, debt was not unknown either. There came a time when Joseph's money from India stopped coming through, and the Sedleys could no longer pay their bills. The knowledge was kept from Amelia for quite a while, though anxiety about their debts made old Mrs Sedley sharp-tongued and bitter, and often critical of Amelia's efforts at kindness and of her pride in her child.

Georgy was now a schoolboy, though it had given Amelia great pain to release him from her care, to mix with rough boys and to be scolded by stern schoolteachers. It was a little local school (run by a friend of Amelia's constant admirer, Mr Linton), and Georgy loved it, doing well at all his lessons and coming home in the evenings with boastful stories of this and that – all of which were believed by his fond mother.

Miss Dobbin followed Georgy's progress with interest, and was keen to be helpful, well aware how poor the Sedleys were.

'Do let Georgy spend the day with me next Saturday,' she said to Amelia one day. 'Miss Osborne is coming to visit, and I know she'd love to see her brother's son. And who knows, perhaps the boy's grandfather will do something for him one day.'

There was a long friendship between the Dobbin and Osborne families. The younger Osborne sister was now married, but the elder, Miss Jane Osborne, still lived at home with her father, old Mr Osborne, whose violent temper and black moods had grown worse year by year since his son's death at Waterloo. Miss Osborne led a sad, gloomy life, and was always asking her friend Miss Dobbin for news of her young nephew.

The meeting took place, and Georgy charmed his aunt, as he did all the women in his life. Miss Osborne, at the dinner table with her father that night, could not hide her emotion.

'What's the matter?' old Mr Osborne growled at last.

Georgy's aunt burst into tears. 'Oh sir,' she said. 'I've seen little George. He's such a beautiful boy – and so like his father!'

The old man did not say a word, but his hands trembled, and he sat staring at the table for a long time.

Soon Georgy told his mother about another visitor at the house on a day he spent with Miss Dobbin.

'An old gentleman came today,' the boy said. 'He watched when I had my riding lesson with Miss Dobbin's coachman. He had very thick eyebrows, and he stared and stared at me.'

Then Amelia knew that the boy had seen his grandfather, and she waited fearfully to see what would happen next.

It was a visit from a lawyer, with a letter from Mr Osborne, read aloud in the lawyer's dry voice.

'Mr Osborne offers to take his grandson George, who will then inherit the fortune which would have gone to his father. He will also give Mrs Amelia Osborne a regular allowance, to enable her and her family to live in comfort. If she marries again, as is said to be likely, this allowance will still continue. In return, the boy will live with Mr Osborne, who will permit him to visit his mother occasionally in her own home.'

Amelia was rarely angry, but today she stood up, tore this letter into a hundred pieces, and threw them on the floor.

'Marry again! Take money – to part from my child! Who dares to insult me in this way? Tell Mr Osborne it is a cowardly letter. I will not answer it. Good day, sir!'

Her parents were not present at this interview, and nothing was said at the time. But it soon became clearer than ever that there were financial difficulties. Dinners became smaller and meaner; both the old people wore worried frowns all the time.

The widow's pension that Amelia received (which, unknown to her, had been increased by payments from Dobbin) was not large. Amelia had always paid part of it to her parents, but this left little to spend on Georgy. And Georgy must have presents. Georgy must have a new suit every Christmas. Georgy must have everything that other boys at the school had.

At Christmas Georgy complained loudly at not having a new suit. Desperate to please him, Amelia sold Dobbin's Indian shawl in order to buy Georgy some books he wanted.

Mrs Sedley saw her putting the new books on Georgy's table. 'What are those?' she said.

'Books for Georgy,' Amelia said. 'I promised them to him.'

'Books!' cried the old lady. 'Books! When we need food!'

'Oh, mother, I – I sold my Indian shawl to get the money.'

'I've had to sell everything I own,' her mother said furiously, 'just to pay the rent, and to keep your dear father out of prison. Jos hasn't sent us any money for months and months, and now you buy books – *books*! – for your son.'

'Oh, mother, mother! Why didn't you tell me?'

'You're too selfish to care about anyone except your son! And he could be rich – he could have whatever he wants, but you will not part with him.' Mrs Sedley was now crying bitterly. 'Amelia, you break my heart!'

'I'll give you everything, mother, all the money I have!'

She fetched all her little store of money, pushed it into her mother's hand, and ran weeping back to her room.

How selfish she had been! One word from her, and Georgy could be rich, and she could save her parents. But she could not bear it, no, no . . . she could not bear to lose her son.

She tried every way she could think of to earn some money,

but she had no skills, and every attempt failed. She wrote to Jos in India, begging him to continue sending money to her parents. One night, finding her father alone and sad in the sitting-room, she tried to comfort him by telling him she had written to Jos, but her father's face turned white with terror.

'It's no good, Emmy my dear,' he whispered. 'Jos still sends the money to his agent in London, but it has to go straight to the money-lender, to pay back all the money I borrowed.' He turned his face away from her. 'You'll hate your old father now.'

'Oh, no, papa!' Amelia threw her arms around him. 'You are always good and kind. You tried your best. It's not the money, it's just that – that . . .' She kissed him wildly, and ran away.

It was over. The battle was lost, the boy must go from her – to others, to forget her. Her joy, hope, love, her whole life. She must give him up.

It all seemed to happen very quickly. Letters were written, arrangements made, legal documents signed. Georgy himself was pleased and excited by the change, boasting to the boys at school that he was going to be rich and live in a big house and have a carriage and a horse and would buy cakes for all his friends.

So Georgy left his mother, with a cheerful smile on his face, and a promise to come and see her often.

Poor Amelia! Nobody really understood the misery she felt at giving away her son: not her parents, nor her friends, and certainly not Miss Dobbin, who wrote to her brother with this and other news – though where she got the other news from was not at all clear.

When this letter arrived in India, Dobbin left it unopened for a few days because his sister's letters usually depressed him. She was always getting her facts wrong, and it was not long ago that he had received Amelia's letter congratulating him on his future marriage. This had upset him deeply, and alone and sleepless in the hot Indian night, he had spoken out loud to her in his room.

'Good God, Amelia! Don't you know that I only love you in the world? You, whom I cared for through months of illness and sorrow, and who said goodbye to me with a smile on your face, and forgot me before the door shut behind me!'

These were not happy memories, but returning to his rooms late one evening, Dobbin decided he must open his sister's letter.

MY DEAR WILLIAM – Have you heard the news about your old friend, Mrs Osborne? Her son Georgy, a fine boy though very spoiled, has gone to live with his grandfather, Mr Osborne. Amelia is probably not too unhappy about giving him up as she is about to marry again – a doctor's assistant, I believe. Not a very good marriage, but Mrs O. is not as young as she was . . .

Dobbin threw the letter down and rushed out of the house. A few minutes later he was banging on his commander's door.

'Colonel!' he shouted. 'I must have permission to leave!'

A window opened above him, and the Colonel's head looked out. He was a good-hearted Irishman, popular with his men.

'What is it, Dob, my boy? Is there a fire? What is it?'

'I must go back to England,' Dobbin shouted. 'On the most urgent private business! I must leave tonight!'

Colonel Crawley's troubles

Rawdon went with the three men who arrested him without argument. He knew that if the money was paid, he would be released from prison the next day.

'How much is it for?' he asked the men.

'Only a small amount,' the first man replied. 'A hundred and seventy pounds. Bills for Mr Nathan.'

The third man went to call a cab to take them to the prison. Rawdon was not too anxious. 'It's not a lot,' he thought. 'Becky can find that much quite easily. But she'll be asleep by now. Let her have her sleep. I'll write to her in the morning.'

Early on Saturday, he sent this letter by messenger.

DEAR BECKY, – I HOPE you slept well. As I was walking home last night, I was arrested for Nathan's bills – a hundred and seventy. Take my watch and anything you can spare and sell them to raise the money. Please do it soon, as tomorrow's Sunday and I don't want to spend another night here. I'm glad it's not Rawdy's weekend for coming home. Yours, R. (Please hurry.)

It would only take three hours, he thought, before Becky would arrive with the money and open his prison doors. But the day passed and no messenger came, and no Becky. It was not until the evening that this letter was delivered.

MY POOR DEAREST LOVE, – I could not sleep at all last night because of worrying over what had happened to you. In the morning I felt so ill that I sent for the doctor, who gave me some medicine to help me sleep, and said I must not be disturbed. So your messenger spent *hours* waiting. You can imagine how I felt

Rawdon went with the men who arrested him without argument.

when I finally read your letter. I got ready at once to go out, but then Lord Steyne arrived with some friends (they were so full of compliments about last night!).

I was *desperate* for them to go and when at last they did, I went down on my knees to Lord Steyne and begged him to give me two hundred pounds. He was in a great fury – but finally he went away, promising to send me the money in the morning, when I will bring it at once to my poor old prisoner – with a kiss from his affectionate Becky. (P.S. I am writing in bed. Oh, I have such a headache, and such a heartache!)

When Rawdon read this letter, his face turned red with anger, and all his suspicions returned. She could not even go out and sell a few things to free him. She could talk about compliments paid to her while he was in prison. Who had put him there? He could hardly bear to think of what he suspected. Quickly, he sat down and wrote a short note to Sir Pitt or Lady Crawley. He begged them to help him, for the sake of his child.

An hour later, he was told he had a visitor. It was Lady Jane. 'Pitt was out when your note arrived,' she said, 'so I came myself.'

Rawdon was so moved by her kind voice that he ran to her, and threw his arms round her, gasping out his thanks.

The debt was quickly paid, and Rawdon thanked Lady Jane again and again, as the carriage took them home. It was nine o'clock at night. He left Lady Jane at her house, and walked and ran through the streets until he arrived breathless outside his own door. Trembling, he stopped and stared up at the house. Lights shone brightly from the drawing-room windows. She had said that she was in bed and ill. He stood there for some time, the light from the rooms on his pale face.

He took out his door key, let himself into the house, and went silently up the stairs. Everywhere was quiet; all the servants had been sent away. He heard laughter in the drawing-room – laughter and singing. Becky was singing. And a voice shouted, 'Well done! Well done!' It was Lord Steyne's.

Rawdon opened the door and went in. There was a little table with dinner for two – and wine. Lord Steyne was leaning over the sofa on which Becky was sitting. She wore her finest evening dress, and around her neck sparkled the diamonds which Steyne had given her. He had her hand in his, and was bowing over it to kiss it, when Becky jumped up with a faint scream as she caught sight of Rawdon's white face. She tried to smile, and Steyne stood up, pale, and with fury in his face.

He attempted a laugh, and came forward, holding out his hand. 'What, you're back? How are you, Crawley?' he said.

The expression on Rawdon's face made Becky throw herself in front of him. 'I am innocent, Rawdon,' she said. 'Before God, I am innocent!' She turned to Lord Steyne. 'Say I am innocent!' she cried.

He thought a trap had been laid for him, and was as furious with the wife as with the husband. 'You – innocent! Damn you!' he screamed. 'You – innocent! Why, every jewel on your body has been paid for by me! I have given you thousands of pounds which your husband has spent, and for which he has sold you! Don't think you can frighten me. Let me pass.'

Rawdon seized him by the neck. 'You lie!' he cried. 'You lie, you cowardly devil!' He struck the noble Lord twice across the face, and threw him, bleeding, to the ground. Unable to stop him, Becky stood there trembling. She admired her husband, strong, brave, and victorious.

'Come here,' Rawdon said. Becky came at once.

'Take off those jewels.' She took them off, still trembling.

Rawdon took the diamonds and threw them at Lord Steyne.

'Come upstairs,' Rawdon said to his wife.

'Don't kill me, Rawdon,' she said.

He laughed angrily. 'I want to see if that man lies about the money as he has about me. Has he given you any?'

'No,' said Becky, 'that is—'

'Give me your keys,' Rawdon said, and they went out together.

Becky had kept back the key to her secret little desk, but Rawdon searched long and hard, and in the end she was forced to open her desk too. It contained love letters, jewellery, and bank-notes – including a new one for a thousand pounds.

'Did he give you this?' Rawdon said.

'Yes,' Becky answered.

'I'll send it back to him today,' said Rawdon. 'And I'll pay Miss Briggs, who was kind to the boy, and some of the debts. You might have sent me a hundred pounds, Becky, out of all this. I have always shared with you.'

'I am innocent,' Becky said. And he left her without another word.

What were her thoughts when he left her? She sat for hours, with the sunlight now pouring into the room. She had heard the door bang as her husband left. She knew he would never come back. He was gone for ever. Would he kill himself? No, not until he had fought Lord Steyne. She thought of all her past life – how comfortless it seemed, how miserable, lonely, and pointless.

When Rawdon arrived at his brother's house in Great Gaunt Street, he was shown into the study to wait. As the clock struck nine, Sir Pitt came into the room, fresh and clean, a model of neatness. He stared in surprise when he saw poor Rawdon, red-eyed and unshaven, with untidy hair.

'Good Heavens, Rawdon!' he said. 'What are you doing here? Why aren't you at home?'

'Home!' said Rawdon, with a wild laugh. 'Pitt, I'm finished.'

'I warned you. I always said this would happen,' his brother answered. 'I can't give you any more money, Rawdon.'

'It's not money I want,' Rawdon said. 'It's the boy I'm worried about. Promise me that when I'm gone you'll take him. Your wife has always been kind to him. My marriage is over.'

'Good God! Is she dead?' Sir Pitt said, in concern.

'I wish *I* was,' said Rawdon. 'If there wasn't my son to worry about, I'd have killed myself this morning, and that devil too.'

Sir Pitt immediately guessed the truth, and that the 'devil' Rawdon wanted to kill was Lord Steyne. Rawdon told his brother the story, and went on, 'There has to be a fight. I attacked him, so he must have his chance of revenge. And I may be killed. Will you and Jane take care of the boy, Pitt? It would comfort me to know that,' he added, in a broken voice.

Sir Pitt was deeply moved, and shook his brother's hand. 'Of course, Rawdon, of course. You have my word on it.'

The money for Miss Briggs was not forgotten, and Rawdon gave it to Pitt. 'Please see that she gets it,' he said. 'I've always felt ashamed of taking the poor old woman's money.'

Rawdon went next to see his friend, Captain Macmurdo, to ask him to make the arrangements for the fight. 'I'm going to kill him, Mac,' Rawdon said. 'There's only one way out of it. They had me arrested. I found them alone together. I told him he was a liar and a coward, and knocked him down and beat him.'

'Good thing too,' Macmurdo said. 'Who is it?'

Rawdon told him.

'Steyne! Good God! He's a friend of the Prince. But – she may be innocent, after all,' Macmurdo said.

'No,' said Rawdon. He took out the thousand-pound note he had found in Becky's desk. 'He gave her this, Mac, and she hid it. She had all this money in the house, and she didn't come and rescue me when I was locked up for debt. You don't know how much I loved her. I sacrificed everything for her.'

The Captain sighed, and agreed to make the arrangements.

When Becky finally shook off her mood of black despair, it was late in the morning. She rang the bell for the servants, again and again, but no one came. In the end she went downstairs and found several people in the drawing-room. The landlord, the landlord's wife, the cook, and several other servants were sitting there, complaining loudly and drinking wine.

Becky was furious. 'How dare you!' she screamed at them. 'How dare you sit on my sofas, drinking my wine!'

'*Your* sofa, indeed!' said the cook. 'I'm sitting on a sofa that belongs to your landlord, like everything else in this house!'

Every servant in the house knew what had happened, and that Becky was finished. They knew she had no money, and could not pay them their long-overdue wages. Some of them had already left, taking valuables with them. Becky's French maid had taken the jewellery left lying on the drawing-room floor, together with all the silver spoons and several of Becky's fine dresses.

The landlord was almost weeping. 'Where's my rent, Mrs Crawley, eh? You've ruined me! I've known the Crawley family all my life. I never thought that one of them would ruin me!'

Becky promised to pay them all the next day, and hurried out of the house. She walked quickly through the streets (she had no money to pay for a carriage) to Sir Pitt's house in Great Gaunt Street. Where was Lady Jane Crawley? It was Sunday, she was at church. And Sir Pitt? In his study. Becky slipped past the servant and was in Sir Pitt's room before her astonished brother-in-law had even laid down his newspaper.

He turned red, and moved back from her with a look of great alarm and horror.

'Don't look at me like that,' Becky said. 'I am not guilty, dear Pitt. You must believe me! You were my friend once. Oh, how could this happen just when I had such good news – just when all our problems were going to be ended.'

'Is it true, then, what I read in the paper?' said Sir Pitt. He had just read a paragraph that had surprised him greatly.

'Yes, it's true. Lord Steyne told me on Friday night that as soon as the news arrived of the death of the previous Governor, he obtained the position for my husband. Rawdon will be the new Governor of Coventry Island! But I had to wait until the announcement was official. And then Rawdon came home . . .'

And so she went on with her persuasive story, pouring it into the ears of her confused brother-in-law. Yes, she had money of which Rawdon knew nothing. But Pitt knew what his brother was like, knew how careless he was about money, how he would have spent it on horses and gambling . . .

'I did it all for my dear husband,' she cried. 'Lord Steyne liked me, yes, and I tried hard, in every honest way I could, to please him. But it was for Rawdon – and you! I wanted him to get Rawdon a good position – I wanted him to make you a lord. Oh, Pitt, dear Pitt, pity me! Bring Rawdon back to me!'

As she spoke, she threw herself down on her knees and, weeping passionately, seized Pitt's hand and kissed it.

It was at that moment that Lady Jane, returning from church, came into the room. She was pale with anger.

'How dare Mrs Crawley enter this house?' she said. 'She's a wicked woman – a heartless mother, a false wife!'

'My love!' cried Sir Pitt. 'You do Rebecca an injustice . . .'

'I have been a faithful and obedient wife to you, Pitt,' Lady Jane continued, 'but I will not have that woman in my house. If she enters it, I and my children will leave it. You must choose, sir, between her and me.' And with that, she walked out of the room, leaving Becky and Sir Pitt astonished by her strong words.

'It was the diamond bracelet you gave me,' Becky said sadly. And before she left him, Sir Pitt had promised to find Rawdon and do all he could to persuade him to forgive his wife.

༄

Lord Steyne refused to challenge Colonel Crawley to a duel. He sent a friend to talk to Captain Macmurdo, and the friend explained that Lord Steyne was innocent, Mrs Crawley was innocent; that he and his wife had also been invited to Curzon Street on that fatal evening but had failed to come owing to his wife's headache; and finally, that the proof of Lord Steyne's friendship for Colonel Crawley was demonstrated beyond question by the appointment of Colonel Crawley as the new Governor of Coventry Island.

Rawdon still wanted to fight, but Captain Macmurdo said no.

'Don't be a fool, man,' he said. 'You've knocked Steyne down and beaten him already. It's my belief your wife's innocent. I think you should take the appointment and hold your tongue.'

So there was no duel between the two men. The thousand-pound note was sent back to Lord Steyne, and after long, hard persuasion from his friends, Rawdon finally agreed to accept the position of Governor of Coventry Island. The climate on the island was said to be very unhealthy – the previous Governor had died after only eighteen months there – but the salary was excellent, and Rawdon would be free of debt for the first time in many long years.

Sir Pitt tried hard to bring Rawdon and Becky together again. He pointed out to his brother all the arguments that supported Becky's story, and stated his own belief in her innocence.

But Rawdon would not hear of it. 'She's been hiding money from me for ten years,' he said. 'She swore that night that she had received no money from Steyne. She knew it was all over, as soon as I found it. If she's not guilty, Pitt, she's as bad as guilty; and I'll never see her again – never.' His head sank down on his chest as he said this, and he looked quite broken and sad.

True to his word, Rawdon left for Coventry Island without forgiving Becky, and young Rawdy went home to Sir Pitt and Lady Jane at Queen's Crawley in the school holidays, where he was very happy. His father wrote to him by every mail.

His mother never made any attempt to see him. Was she guilty or not? Everybody knows that Vanity Fair is never kind with its verdicts in these matters. Rawdon's lawyers paid her enough money to live on, and people said she had gone to Europe, but where she lived, or how she lived, no one knew – or cared.

10

Major Dobbin returns from India

Georgy Osborne enjoyed his new life at his grandfather's house in Russell Square. His good looks and bright, cheerful nature pleased the old man very much, and Mr Osborne was soon as proud of his grandson as he had been of his son.

The boy had many more luxuries and comforts than had been given to his father. Mr Osborne's wealth had increased greatly in recent years, and he had ambitious plans for his grandson, who was sent to an expensive little school, and who wore the finest clothes any young gentleman was ever seen in – even his shirts had little jewelled buttons. The neat, plain shirts that his mother had sewn for him with such loving care were never worn – Miss Osborne gave them to the coachman's boy.

In Russell Square everybody was afraid of Mr Osborne, and Mr Osborne was afraid of Georgy, who ruled his new home like a king. He was clever and better educated than his grandfather, and had little respect for the old man, whose manners were rude and rough. Mr Osborne spoiled Georgy, admired him, and laughed with delight at his commanding ways.

'Did you ever see a boy like him?' he would often say. 'Drinks his wine at dinner like a lord! Oh, he's a fine little gentleman!'

After breakfast, Georgy would sit in the armchair reading the newspaper, just like a grown-up man. He even had his personal servant, who would bring him his letters on a silver tray.

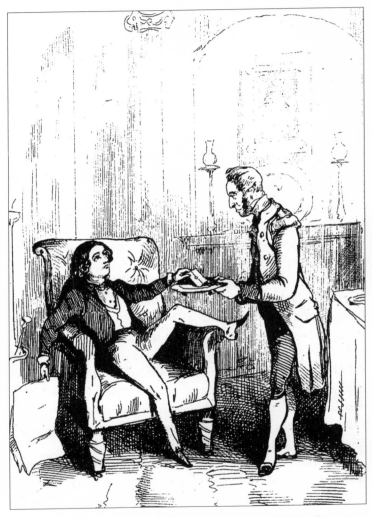

*Georgy even had his personal servant, who would bring him
his letters on a silver tray.*

But despite all this, Georgy was still a good-natured boy, and still fond of his mother. On one of his regular visits he eagerly pulled a red leather case out of his pocket and gave it to her.

'I bought it with my own money, mama,' he said. 'I thought you'd like it.'

Amelia opened the case, and giving a cry of delight, seized the boy and covered him with kisses. It was a miniature painting of Georgy. His grandfather had had a painting of the boy done by a famous artist, and Georgy asked the artist to make a little copy of the painting. It made Amelia so happy, this little picture. She wept and laughed over it, slept with it under her pillow, and kissed it a hundred times a day.

There was little else in her life to give her much joy. Not long after Georgy went to live with Mr Osborne, Mrs Sedley fell ill. She was a difficult patient, but Amelia was always at her bedside, always ready with a gentle answer to that complaining voice, always offering a daughter's loving kindness in exchange for the hard words she received.

When they had buried the old lady, Amelia's father became totally dependent on his daughter. He was a sad old man, with a shaky memory, his mind often wandering in the past, but Amelia did everything she could to make her old father happy. And so the days went by, with Georgy's visits the only bright points in Amelia's dull, dutiful life.

❧

Major Dobbin had easily obtained permission from his good-natured commander to return to England. He travelled night and day across country to the port, where he was struck down by a fever that nearly killed him. He lay at the edge of death for a long time, and it was many, many weeks before he was able to take the ship for home. He was as thin as a stick and as weak as a baby, but the long sea journey gave him back his health and strength.

The journey also gave him a most unexpected companion – no other than Joseph Sedley, the brother of the woman whose name Dobbin had murmured so often during his long illness.

Our old friend Jos, after ten years with the East India Company, was sailing home, richer, but otherwise unchanged. Many a night, as the ship was cutting through the roaring dark sea, the moon and stars shining overhead, Jos and the Major would sit talking of home. And with great skill and cunning the Major always brought the talk round to the subject of Amelia.

'I hope,' he said once, 'she will be happy in her new marriage.'

'Marriage?' said Jos. 'Her last letter to me said nothing about marriage. She wrote to say that *you* were going to be married, and she hoped that *you* would be happy.'

It was wonderful to see after this, how bright and cheerful the Major became, and how quickly he recovered his strength.

They landed in England at Southampton, late at night, but very early the next morning Dobbin banged at Jos's door.

'Sedley,' he called. 'Time to go. The carriage is ready.'

A bad-tempered growl greeted him, and Mr Sedley informed the Major that the Major could go to the devil or wherever he pleased, but that he, Jos, would finish his sleep in peace.

So Dobbin travelled to London alone, and made his way to the Sedleys' house. At the door he began to tremble. 'Suppose she is married, after all,' he thought. 'Suppose she's moved.'

A girl of about sixteen opened the door.

Dobbin was as pale as a ghost. 'Does Mrs Osborne live here?'

The girl stared at him, and then her face went white. 'Oh! Oh!' she cried. 'It's Major Dobbin! Do you remember me? I'm Mary

– the landlord's daughter. I was only little when you went away.'

Yes, of course the Major remembered Mary Clapp, who used to play with Georgy as a baby. And Mrs Osborne . . .? She was walking in the park, he was told, with her poor old father. The Major would like to see her – would Mary show him the way?

'I'll get my hat at once,' said Mary, delighted.

Mary took Dobbin's arm, and as they walked, she answered all the Major's many questions about Mrs Osborne. Yes, she was very unhappy about parting with her son. No, she never had any gentlemen visitors. And Mary heard the Major's sigh of relief when she said this, and she felt the Major's arm jump under her hand as he caught sight of Amelia in the park. Oh yes, Mary Clapp knew all there was to know about the Major's heart.

She ran ahead to find Amelia.

'News, news!' she cried. 'He's come, he's come!'

'Who's come?' Amelia called, jumping up in alarm.

Then she saw Dobbin's tall figure approaching; she turned white, then red, and began – naturally – to cry. She ran towards him, holding out her hands, smiling through her tears.

Dobbin looked at her lovingly. She had not changed. The same kind eyes, and soft brown hair. She looked up at his plain, honest face, and he took her two little hands between his, and held them there. Why did he not take her in his arms, and swear that he would never leave her? She would have accepted, surely.

After a pause he said, 'Someone else has come with me.'

'Mrs Dobbin?' she said, moving back. Why didn't he speak?

'No,' he said, letting her hands go. 'Who has told you those lies? I mean, your brother Jos. He came in the same ship with me, and has come home to make you all happy.'

'Papa!' Amelia cried. 'Jos is home! And here's Major Dobbin!'

Mr Sedley was confused and worried by all this excitement, but he recognized Dobbin and was pleased to see him. They all returned to the house, and Dobbin stayed for hours, drinking endless cups of tea, and watching that dear, remembered face.

Amelia talked only of Georgy, what a wonderful, intelligent, handsome, delightful boy he was. Such a joy and comfort to his mother – and so like his dear father who was gone.

Dobbin watched as Amelia put her handkerchief to her eyes. 'Should I be angry with her,' he thought, 'for being so faithful to George? Can that heart love only once and for ever?'

When Joseph Sedley arrived the next day, he was shocked to see how sorrow and misfortune had changed his father. The old man wept as he told his son about his wife's death, and the hard times they had all lived through. And in the emotion of that first meeting, Jos swore that he would take care of them from now on; that his house and everything he had would be theirs; and that Amelia would look very pretty at the head of his dinner table – until, of course, she accepted one of her own.

Amelia shook her head sadly and, as usual, began to cry. She knew what he meant. She and her young friend Mary Clapp had talked over the subject very fully after the Major's visit.

'Didn't you see,' Mary said, 'how he shook all over when you asked if he was married, and he said, "Who told you those lies?" Oh, Mrs O., he never took his eyes off you for a second! I'm sure he's gone grey-haired with thinking about you all these years.'

'Mary, you mustn't say such things. I love him as a brother, but a woman who has been married to *him*' – Amelia pointed to George's picture on the wall above her bed – 'can never think of another marriage.'

Poor Mary sighed, and felt rather sorry for Major Dobbin.

It had been Dobbin on the long voyage home who had made Jos promise to take care of his family, and this time Jos kept his promise. One day his carriage came to the house and carried his father and sister away to live in comfort once more.

Dobbin was there to meet them when they arrived with their possessions, which included the old piano, rescued long ago by Dobbin himself from the sale at the Sedleys' former house.

Dobbin was very pleased to see the piano. 'I'm glad you've kept it,' he said. 'I didn't think you cared about it.'

'Of course I do,' Amelia replied. '*He* gave it to me.'

'Oh, I didn't know,' said poor Dobbin, looking very sad.

Later, thinking about Dobbin's sad face, Amelia realized that it must have been Dobbin who gave her the piano, not George. She had loved it all these years because it was George's gift. But it was not George's gift after all. So now it meant nothing to her. But she was sorry if she had hurt Dobbin's feelings.

'I have to beg your pardon for something,' she said to him a few days later. 'I never thanked you for the piano when you gave it to me. I thought that it came from someone else. Thank you, William.' She held out her hand, and her eyes filled with tears.

Dobbin could bear no more.

'Amelia, Amelia!' he cried, 'I have loved you since the day I first saw you. For twelve years you have never been out of my thoughts. I came to tell you I loved you before I went to India, but you didn't care whether I stayed or went, so I didn't speak.'

'I was very ungrateful,' said Amelia.

'No; you didn't care. I understand how you feel about the piano. You're sorry that it came from me, and not from George. I'm a fool for thinking that years of love could matter to you.'

'Now you are being cruel,' Amelia said. 'George is my husband still. How could I love another? I loved you like a brother, and a dear, true, kind friend. I thought you might have saved me from that dreadful parting from my son – which nearly killed me. You didn't come, but you are still my friend, his friend and mine.' Her voice broke and she hid her face on his shoulder.

The Major held her gently, kissing her head as if she was a child. 'I will not change, dear Amelia,' he said. 'I ask for no more than your love. Only let me stay near you and see you often.'

'Yes, often,' Amelia said.

And that was all Dobbin had – permission to be near her and to see her, and nothing more.

❧

Life was now much more comfortable for Amelia, but there were more changes ahead. In the winter Mr Sedley died, cared for devotedly by Amelia in his last illness, and less than a year later, Mr Osborne was found dead in his bedroom one morning.

The old man had softened in his last year and, under Dobbin's influence, his anger and hate had faded away. He had left half his fortune to Georgy, and half to his two daughters. But there was also a pension of five hundred pounds a year for Amelia. And he wished his grandson to return to the care of his mother, the widow of his much loved son.

Amelia was overjoyed, and when she learnt it was Dobbin who had caused the change of heart in the old man, she was deeply grateful to him – deeply grateful, but no more. If she thought of anything else, a picture of George rose before her eyes and said, 'You are mine, and mine only, now and for ever.'

A meeting with an old friend

Fortune now began to smile on Amelia. It was amazing how differently people behaved towards her as soon as they heard that Mr Osborne had left money to her. She found that everyone treated her with respect, that the servants were more attentive to her instructions, and that she suddenly had a wide circle of affectionate friends. Even Jos, who used to treat her as a harmless poor relation whom it was his duty to look after, became quite respectful and anxious to please her.

Major Dobbin, who was now Georgy's guardian, often took the boy out, and the two became firm friends. Georgy admired and respected the Major and, anxious to win his approval, became less boastful and selfish in his own behaviour.

'I like him because he knows so much,' he said to his mother, 'and he never boasts about all the things he's done.'

When summer came, Joseph Sedley decided that a trip to Europe would be an agreeable way of passing the time, and his sister and nephew were delighted with the plan. So they took the boat from London to Germany, accompanied of course by Major Dobbin, as a close family friend.

For weeks they travelled through the towns along the banks of the river Rhine, visiting the sights, and enjoying themselves in their different ways. After a large lunch, Jos usually read the newspapers (or fell asleep over them), while the others went on excursions. Amelia was fond of drawing, and sat in the sunshine, drawing castles and churches. Sometimes they climbed up to a ruined tower on a hill-top, where Georgy ran about exploring, and Amelia drew the view. Dobbin carried her little chair and her sketch-book, and admired the drawings as they had never been admired before. Perhaps it was the happiest time of both their lives, if they had only known it. But who does?

When they came to the little town of Pumpernickel, Jos liked it so much that he decided to stay there for the winter. They rented a pleasant house, and were welcomed into local society, receiving invitations to parties, dinners and balls.

On one occasion the wedding of a local German prince took place. The town was full of visitors for the celebrations, and everybody was invited to a grand ball. Jos and his party went, including young Georgy, who watched the dancing for a while, but then got bored, and wandered away through the other rooms in search of better entertainment.

He found himself in the gambling rooms, with the card tables and the roulette wheel, a place where his guardian the Major would never normally let him enter. But Georgy was fascinated, and stood close to the roulette table, watching the gamblers as they played, and won . . . and lost . . . and lost again.

One of them, a lady with light hair, in a low-necked dress and wearing a black mask, kept on losing. She looked around, saw Georgy watching, and stared at him.

'You never play, sir?' she said in a French accent.

'No, madame,' the boy replied.

'Will you do something for me, then?' she said.

'What is it?' said Georgy, blushing a little.

'Play this for me, please. Put it on any number you like.'

She took a gold coin from her purse, the only coin there, and gave it to him. The boy laughed, and did as she asked.

And his number won. It always does, they say, for beginners.

'Thank you,' the lady said, pulling a pile of money towards her. 'Thank you. What is your name?'

'My name's George Osborne,' said the boy.

*Dobbin admired Amelia's drawings
as they had never been admired before.*

At this moment the Major and Jos appeared, looking for him. Dobbin took Georgy's arm and quickly led him away. He looked back over his shoulder at Jos, who was watching with interest as the masked lady won on the next spin of the roulette wheel.

'Are you coming with us?' Dobbin asked him.

'You go on,' Jos replied. 'I'll follow in a while.'

Outside the room Dobbin said to George, 'Did you play?' The boy said, 'No.'

'Give me your promise that you never will,' said Dobbin.

'Why?' Georgy said. 'It seems very good fun.'

In a serious voice Dobbin explained why Georgy should never gamble. He did not mention, of course, how Georgy's own father had demonstrated the foolishness of gambling.

Jos remained behind. He was no gambler, but he liked a little excitement now and then, and he had some coins in his pocket. He put one down over the fair shoulder of the masked lady, and they won. She gently tapped the empty chair next to her.

'Come and give me good luck,' she said.

Jos sat down, murmuring confused compliments.

'I play to forget, but I cannot,' said the mask. 'I cannot forget old times, sir. Your little nephew is so like his father. And you – you have not changed – but yes, you have. Everybody changes, everybody forgets; nobody has any heart.'

'Good God, who is it?' cried Jos, alarmed.

'Can't you guess, Joseph Sedley?' said the little woman, taking off her mask and looking at him. 'You have forgotten me.'

'Good heavens! Mrs Crawley!' gasped Jos.

'Rebecca,' she said, putting her hand on his. 'I'm staying at the Elephant Hotel. Ask for Madame de Raudon. I saw my dear Amelia today. How pretty she looked, and how happy! So do you! Everybody is happy, except me. I am so miserable, Joseph Sedley.'

She played another coin on the black. Her eyes followed the wheel as it spun, but the red won, and she lost her money.

'Come with me for a little while,' she said to Jos. 'We are old friends, aren't we, dear Mr Sedley?'

What had happened to Mrs Rebecca Crawley in the two years since that dreadful night in Curzon Street? She went first to Boulogne on the French coast, where she led a quiet, respectable life for a while. But of the many English travellers passing through, there were always some who knew her story. And then the gossip began; society ladies would ignore her, and the men would laugh at her, or be too familiar, even insulting. One young man, who in London used to walk a mile through the rain to find her carriage for her, tried to force his way into her sitting-room, and she had to shut the door in his face.

It made her feel very lonely. 'If *he* had been here,' she thought, 'those cowards would never dare to insult me.' She thought about 'him' with great sadness – his honest, stupid kindness, his good humour, his faithfulness and obedience, his bravery. And perhaps she cried a little too.

She moved on to Ostend, Florence, Rome . . . Through his lawyers, Rawdon was paying her three hundred pounds a year, on the condition that she never troubled him again. But when she got her money, she gambled; when she had gambled it, she had to live as best she could. Some said she gave singing lessons, and sang in theatres. Certainly, the Elephant Hotel in Pumpernickel, where Joseph Sedley visited her the next day, was full of actors and entertainers and noisy young students. Becky liked the life.

She was, after all, the daughter of an artist and a dancer, and was happy to drink brandy-and-water and share a joke with anyone.

Meeting Joseph Sedley again, though, offered Becky a chance, which she seized with both hands. She had charmed him before; she could charm him again. When he arrived, she welcomed him into her little room with tearful delight, and he listened in shock and horror to the terrible story that Becky poured into his ears – the ill-treatment and injustice and cruelty that she had suffered.

He hurried back home to tell Amelia all about it. 'She's so miserable, Emmy,' he said. 'She hasn't a friend in the world.'

'That woman brings trouble wherever she goes,' Dobbin said.

None of them had heard the gossip about Becky because they had no connections with London high society, but Dobbin remembered certain events in Brussels long ago. Amelia, too, remembered the fear and jealousy that her friend had caused her. A soft, gentle heart, however, is soon moved to sympathy.

'Mrs Crawley has a son, the same age as Georgy,' Jos went on. 'He adores his mother. And they tore him screaming out of her arms, and have never allowed him to see her since.'

Amelia jumped to her feet. 'Dear Jos,' she said. 'The poor, poor woman. William, let's go and see her at once.'

It was lucky that Becky saw them coming from her window, and so was able to hide the brandy bottle under the bed and send away the two young students she had been laughing with.

When Amelia saw Becky, she forgave her at once, and ran forward to kiss her. Becky was truly grateful to her for her kind, generous heart, and although the emotion did not last long, it was real while it lasted. The two women talked in Becky's room for two hours, while Dobbin sat in the hall below, watching the comings and goings in the hotel. He was not impressed by Mrs

Crawley, nor deceived by her, and when they returned to the house and Amelia began to make arrangements for a room for Becky, he became very alarmed.

'You're going to have that woman in the *house*?' he said.

'Of course we are,' said Amelia. 'The poor woman has suffered so much. Of course we are going to have her here.'

'Of course, my dear,' Jos said.

'Her husband deserted her and took her child away from her!' Amelia said. 'I must help her – she's my oldest friend.'

'She was not always your friend, Amelia,' said Dobbin, who was now quite angry.

'Shame on you, Major Dobbin!' Amelia said fiercely.

She went to her room and shut the door. How dare Dobbin insult George's memory? 'You were pure,' she said to the picture above her bed, 'and I was wrong and wicked to be jealous.'

Poor Dobbin! He had just ruined the work of many years. He tried hard to persuade Jos not to receive Mrs Crawley into his home, but they were interrupted by the arrival of the lady herself, with her luggage. She greeted them with great respect, especially Major Dobbin, since she saw at once that he was her enemy. Amelia appeared from her room to welcome Becky and took no notice of the Major, except to give him an angry look.

There were four places as usual at the dinner table that evening, but the fourth place was taken by Rebecca.

'Hello, where's Dob?' Georgy asked when he came in.

'He's eating out, I suppose,' his mother said, pulling her son close to her and kissing him. 'This is my boy, Rebecca,' she said.

Becky looked at Georgy admiringly, and took his hand fondly. 'Dear boy!' she said. 'He is just like my . . .' Emotion prevented her from saying more, but Amelia understood that she was thinking of her own dear child. In spite of all this emotion, however, Becky managed to eat a very good dinner.

Dobbin, angry and hurt at the way Amelia had treated him, went to see an Englishman he knew and asked if the name of Mrs Rawdon Crawley meant anything to him. He was in luck. The man knew all the London gossip, and told the astonished Major the full history of Becky, her husband, and Lord Steyne.

The next morning Dobbin asked to see Amelia, but she would not see him until the afternoon. She greeted him coldly. Becky was also there, and came forward smiling, holding out her hand. Dobbin stepped back from her.

'I am sorry, Mrs Crawley,' he said, 'but I must tell you that I have not come here as your friend.'

'I wonder what Major Dobbin has to say against Rebecca,' said Amelia in a low, clear voice, with a determined look in her eyes.

'Oh, don't let's have any of this,' said Jos, alarmed at the signs of a quarrel. 'I will *not* have this sort of thing in my house.'

'Dear friend,' Rebecca said sweetly, 'please hear what Major Dobbin has to say against me.'

'I will *not* hear it, I say,' Jos said, and he left the room.

'We are only two women,' Amelia said. 'You can speak now.'

'There is no need to behave in this way, Amelia,' said Dobbin. 'I do not usually speak critically of women. It is not a pleasure for me to do what I have to do.'

'Then please do it quickly,' said Amelia impatiently.

'I came to say, Mrs Crawley, I have heard things about you that I do not wish to repeat in front of Mrs Osborne. A woman who is separated from her husband, who travels under a false name, who gambles – is not a suitable companion for Mrs Osborne and her son.'

'Of what exactly are you accusing me, Major Dobbin?' Becky said. 'Unfaithfulness to my husband? I deny it, and no one can prove it because I am innocent. Are you accusing me of being poor, alone, and unhappy? Yes, I am guilty of those faults, and I am punished for them every day. Let me go, Emmy. I shall continue to wander through life alone, being insulted because I am alone. Let me go. The poor wanderer will be on her way. My stay here spoils this gentleman's plans.'

'Indeed it does, and if I have any power in this house . . .'

'Power, none!' cried Amelia. 'Rebecca, you stay with me. I won't desert you because you have suffered. Come away, dear.'

And the two ladies went to the door. Dobbin opened it, but as they were going out, he took Amelia's hand and said, 'Amelia, will you stay a moment and speak to me?'

'He wishes to speak with you when I'm not there,' said Becky unhappily. Amelia held her hand tightly.

'Believe me, it's not about you that I'm going to speak,' Dobbin said. 'Come back, Amelia,' and she came. Dobbin closed the door behind Mrs Crawley. Amelia looked up at him. Her face and her lips were quite white.

'I was confused when I spoke just now,' the Major said, 'and I misused the word "power". I was wrong. But your husband asked me to look after you. That's why I have spoken as I have.'

'Yesterday you insulted his memory. And I will never forgive you – never!' Amelia said, filled with anger and emotion.

'You don't mean that, Amelia,' Dobbin said sadly. 'You don't mean that those few words have more weight than a life-time's devoted love? I have never insulted George, and I don't deserve this from his widow and the mother of his son. I'm sure if you think about it, you will want to take back your accusation.'

Amelia held her head down.

'I have loved and watched you for fifteen years,' he continued, 'and I know now that you can only love a dream. You cannot love as I deserve to be loved, as I would have been loved by a woman more generous than you. I know now that you are not capable of such love. I find no fault with you. You are very good-natured, and have done your best, but you could never love me as I love you. I have waited long enough. I am tired of it. We are both tired of it. Goodbye, Amelia. Let it end at last.'

Amelia stood silent and afraid as Dobbin suddenly broke the chain by which she had held him for so long. She didn't wish to marry him, but she wished to keep him. She wished to give him nothing, but wanted him to give her everything.

'Are you saying that . . . that you're going away, William?' she said.

He gave a sad laugh. 'I went once before,' he said, 'but I came back – after twelve years. We were young then, Amelia. I have spent enough of my life waiting. Goodbye.'

While they had been talking, the door had opened just a crack, and, unknown to them, Becky had listened to every word.

'What a fine man he is,' she thought, 'and how badly she treats him.' She admired Dobbin, and was not bitter because of the things he had said about her. It was an open move in the game, and he had played it fairly. 'Ah, if only I'd had a husband like that,' she thought. She hurried to her room and wrote him a note in which she begged him to wait for a few days, and not to leave because, she said, she could help him with Amelia.

The parting was over. Once more poor William walked to the door and was gone. And the little widow had won her victory, and was left to enjoy it as best she could.

At dinner that evening everyone was silent, and Amelia ate nothing. Afterwards, Georgy was looking out of the window at Dobbin's house, which was opposite.

'Look!' he said. 'They're bringing out Dobbin's carriage and putting his luggage in it. Is he going somewhere?'

'Yes,' his mother replied. 'He's going on a journey.'

'On a journey? When is he coming back?' Georgy asked.

'He's . . . not coming back,' Amelia replied.

'Not coming back!' cried Georgy, jumping up.

'Stay where you are!' shouted Jos.

'Stay, Georgy,' his mother said, with a very sad face.

The boy returned to the window, looking puzzled and uneasy.

When the servants began to say their goodbyes to the Major, Georgy could bear it no longer. 'I *will* go!' he cried.

'Give him this,' said Becky quickly, and passed him a note.

Georgy took it, and rushed out of the house. Dobbin was already in the carriage. Georgy jumped in after him, threw his arms round the Major's neck (as they saw from the window), and began asking him questions. Then he took the note from his pocket and gave it to him. Dobbin opened it, trembling, but then his expression changed, and he tore the note in two and dropped it out of the carriage window. Then he kissed Georgy on the head and the boy got down from the carriage, which at once moved away. Dobbin did not look up as he passed below Amelia's window. And Georgy, left alone in the street, began to cry loudly.

And Amelia? She had her picture of George to comfort her.

12

Births, marriages, and deaths

Becky's plan for helping Major Dobbin to achieve his desire remained a secret, as she was more interested in her own concerns for the moment. Suddenly and unexpectedly, she found herself living in comfort, surrounded by kind, good-natured people, and the change from her usual restless, uncertain life was very pleasant to her.

So, as she was pleased herself, she tried hard to please others. She had always been good at that, and before long Joseph Sedley was her devoted slave and admirer. He stopped falling asleep after dinner. He drove out with Becky in his carriage. He invited people to dinner and gave little parties to entertain her. Soon she had a circle of admirers, and Jos's house had never been so lively as Becky caused it to be. She sang, she played, she laughed, she talked in two or three languages; she brought everybody to the house – and made Jos believe that they came to see *him*.

Becky soon discovered how to please Amelia. She talked to her constantly about Dobbin, how she admired him, and how cruelly Amelia had treated him. Amelia defended herself, saying she owed a lifelong devotion to George, she could never forget him, he had been the best, the most wonderful husband anyone could have . . . But at the same time she seemed to like hearing Becky praise the Major, and indeed, she brought the conversation round to him herself, at least twenty times a day.

She was not happy, though. She was nervous, silent, and hard to please. In the evenings, when she tried to sing the Major's favourite songs, she would break off and hurry to her room, where, no doubt, the picture of her husband would comfort her. Georgy, looking for something in his mother's desk one day, found a pair of the Major's gloves there, neatly folded and placed in one of the secret drawers.

Dobbin wrote regularly to Georgy, and once or twice he wrote to Amelia too, but his letters were cold. She had lost her power over him, and he no longer loved her, she realized. He had left her, and she saw now the beauty and the purity of the affection that she had thrown away, and she was miserable.

In June, they moved to Ostend on the Belgian coast, for the sea air. Becky met some gentlemen friends there, from her travelling days, and although she wasn't pleased to see them, they were very pleased to see her, and to learn that she had a rich friend in Mr Sedley. They invaded Jos's house, ate his dinners, drank his wine, paid drunken compliments to Amelia, and argued which of them should marry the rich little widow.

Becky made sure that Amelia was never left alone with these men, but Amelia was still terrified of them. She begged Jos to take her home to England, but since Becky preferred to stay in Europe, so did Jos. At last, in despair one day, Amelia wrote secretly to a friend. When she returned from posting the letter, she went to her room and stayed there. Becky realized that Amelia was frightened of the visitors in the drawing-room.

'She must go away, the silly little fool,' Becky thought. 'She needs a husband, and she must marry the Major. I'll arrange it tonight.' So she took a cup of tea to Amelia in her room, and found her sitting there with her picture, very sad and nervous.

'Thank you,' said Amelia.

'Listen to me, Amelia,' Becky said, looking at Amelia with a sort of angry kindness. 'You must go away from here and from men like these. They are not good men. Never mind how I know them – I know everybody. Jos can't protect you; he's too weak. He can't even protect himself. And as for you, you are no more able to look after yourself than a baby. You must marry, or you and your precious boy will be ruined. You must have a husband, you fool; and one of the best gentlemen I ever saw has asked you a hundred times, and you have refused him, you silly, heartless, ungrateful little creature!'

'I tried – I tried my best, Rebecca,' said Amelia, sorrowfully, 'but I couldn't forget . . .' and she looked up at the picture of George which was over her bed.

'Couldn't forget *him*!' cried Becky. 'That selfish fool! That vain, boastful, heartless creature! He was tired of you, Amelia, and would never have married you if Dobbin hadn't forced him to keep his promise. George told me. He never cared for you. He used to make fun of you, time after time. And the week after he married you, he was whispering words of love to me.'

'That's not true, Rebecca!' Amelia cried, jumping up.

'Look at this, then, you fool,' said Rebecca, calmly. She took out a little note from her pocket, and dropped it into Amelia's hands. 'You know his writing. He wrote that to me – wanted me to run away with him – gave it to me under your nose, the day before he was shot – which he well deserved!'

Amelia did not hear her; she was looking at the letter. It was the letter that George had hidden in the flowers and given to Becky on the night of the ball before the battle of Waterloo. It was true. George had asked Becky to go away with him.

Amelia put her face in her hands, and wept. Were those tears sweet or bitter? Did she cry because George was no longer the perfect husband she had adored – or because there was now no reason to stop her loving Dobbin? 'There's nothing to forbid me now,' she thought. 'I may love him with all my heart now. Oh, I will, I will, if he will let me, if he will forgive me.'

Indeed, Amelia did not cry as much as Becky expected and, after a moment or two, Becky kissed her and said, 'And now let us write to him this very minute.'

'I – I wrote to him this morning,' Amelia said, blushing.

Becky laughed so loudly that the whole house could hear her.

❧

Two mornings after this, in spite of heavy rain and a strong wind, Amelia rose early and insisted on taking a walk along the harbour with Georgy. They stared anxiously out across the rough sea, with the rain beating in their faces.

'I hope he won't cross in such bad weather,' Amelia said.

'Of course he will,' the boy said. He pointed out to sea. 'Look, mother, there's the ship now!'

Yes, there was the ship, but he might not be on it – he might not have got the letter – he might not choose to come. A hundred fears poured into Amelia's heart. The white-topped waves were beating like thunder against the harbour wall, and no doubt that little heart was beating just as wildly.

The ship came nearer, and a tall, thin figure could be seen on it, staring towards the harbour. 'Look – there he is!' Georgy shouted. 'The man in the greatcoat – it's Dob!' He threw his arms round his mother.

Now the ship was in the harbour, now the tall thin figure was hurrying off the ship. Suddenly, Georgy ran away, to look at something terribly interesting at the other end of the harbour, leaving his mother standing trembling in the rain.

Then she stepped forward, with her two little hands held out before her, and the next minute she had disappeared in his arms.

A little murmur could be heard. 'Forgive – dear William – dear, dear friend – forgive, forgive . . .' She was kissing one of his hands again and again, and with his other hand, Dobbin held her close to his heart, safe within the folds of his greatcoat.

Eventually Amelia lifted her head, and looked up at his face. It was full of sadness and love and pity.

'It was time you sent for me, dear Amelia,' he said.

'You will never leave me again, will you, William?'

'No, never,' he answered, and held her tightly.

At last Dobbin had what he had wanted every day and every hour for eighteen years. There she was, close to his heart, whispering loving words. At last he had the prize he had been hoping for all his life.

They walked to the house, and Georgy danced round them, laughing and singing joyously. And there we will leave them.

❧

Becky never showed herself to Amelia and Dobbin again. Perhaps it was a feeling of guilt towards the kind and simple creature who had been the first in life to defend her. Perhaps it was a dislike of emotional occasions, but she disappeared at once to Bruges on 'particular business', she said; and only Georgy and his uncle were present at the wedding of Major William Dobbin to Mrs Amelia Osborne.

When it was over, and Georgy and his parents had left for England, Becky returned (just for a few days, of course) to comfort poor Jos, who was now left alone. Jos preferred the

European life, he said, and refused his sister's invitation to live with her and her husband in England.

Dobbin left the army after he was married, and he and his family rented a house near Queen's Crawley, where Sir Pitt, Lady Jane, their daughter, and young Rawdon Crawley were living. Sir Pitt's little son, always sickly, had died some years ago, which meant that young Rawdon would be the next baronet.

When Amelia gave birth to a daughter, Dobbin's happiness was complete. Lady Jane and Mrs Dobbin became great friends, and Georgy and young Rawdon played together in the holidays, went to Cambridge University together – and quarrelled about Lady Jane's daughter, with whom they were both in love.

Mrs Rawdon Crawley's name was never mentioned by either family. There were reasons for this silence, because wherever Joseph Sedley went, she went too, and that foolish man seemed to be completely her slave. Dobbin's lawyers informed him that his brother-in-law had taken out a heavy insurance on his life, and had probably been raising money to pay debts.

Hearing about this, Amelia, in great alarm, begged Dobbin to go and see her brother, who was now in Brussels.

Jos was living in a hotel, in which Mrs Crawley also had an apartment, and Jos begged Dobbin to visit him at a time when he believed Becky was out. Dobbin found his brother-in-law in very poor health, and dreadfully afraid of Becky, though eager in his praises of her. She had looked after him devotedly through a number of strange illnesses. She had been a daughter to him.

'But – but – oh, for God's sake, please come and live near me, and – and – see me sometimes,' Jos begged.

Dobbin frowned. 'We can't, Jos,' he said. 'You know Amelia can't visit you while Rebecca is here.'

'You don't know what a terrible woman she is,' poor Jos said.

'But Becky is innocent,' Joseph said desperately. 'Innocent as a child, as innocent as your own wife.'

'That may be so,' Dobbin said, gloomily; 'but Emmy can't visit you while she's here. Be a man, Jos. Break off this connection, and come home to your family. We hear you are in debt too.'

'In debt!' cried Jos. 'Nonsense! Mrs Crawley has – I mean, all my money is quite – is well taken care of.'

'You are not in debt then? Why did you insure your life?'

'I thought – in case anything happened – a little present to her, so grateful . . . but all my money will come to you, of course.'

Dobbin begged Jos to run away, to go back to India where Mrs Crawley could not follow him, to escape while he still could.

Jos seized Dobbin's hand. 'Yes, I'll go to India, but don't tell her. I must have time. She'd kill me if she knew. You don't know what a terrible woman she is,' the poor man said.

'Then why not come away with me now?' Dobbin said.

But Jos did not have the courage to do that. He would see Dobbin again, but Dobbin must say nothing about his visit, and must go now. Becky might come in at any moment. And Dobbin left, full of fear and anxiety.

He never saw Jos again. Three months later Joseph Sedley died in France. Most of his money had gone, except for the insurance money, which was divided equally between his 'sister Amelia' and his 'friend Rebecca'. Lawyers for the insurance company said that it was a most suspicious case, and they wanted an investigation into the death. But 'friend Rebecca' – or Lady Crawley, as she now called herself – came to London at once, and hired her own lawyers. She won the case and the money was paid.

She never was Lady Crawley, though she continued to use the name. Her husband Rawdon died of yellow fever on Coventry

Island, six weeks before the death of his brother, Sir Pitt Crawley. On Sir Pitt's death, Becky's son, as the only living male in the Crawley family, became Sir Rawdon Crawley and inherited all the Crawley houses and land.

Sir Rawdon continues to live at Queen's Crawley with Lady Jane and her daughter. He has refused to see his mother, to whom he pays a generous yearly allowance, and who appears in any case to be very wealthy. She lives in Bath and London, and many people believe her to be a most cruelly treated woman. She has her enemies. Who has not? But she goes to church, and is deeply involved in church events that raise money to help the sick, the poor, the homeless, and other unhappy people.

At one of these events in London, Amelia and her family suddenly came face to face with Becky. She gave an amused little smile as they hurried away from her – Amelia on the arm of her son Georgy, now a handsome young gentleman, and Dobbin, carrying his little daughter Janey, of whom he is fonder than of anything in the world.

'Fonder than he is of me,' Amelia thinks, with a sigh. But he never said a word to Amelia that was not kind and gentle, or thought of a wish of hers that he did not try to satisfy.

Oh, the vanity and folly of human wishes! Which of us is happy in this world? Which of us has our heart's desire? Or, having it, is satisfied?

GLOSSARY

adore to love somebody very much

affection a strong feeling of liking or love; *(adj)* **affectionate**

astonished very surprised

ball a large formal party with dancing

baronet a nobleman who has the title 'Sir' and can pass the title on to his son when he dies

billiards a game for two people played with long sticks and three balls on a long table

blush to become red in the face, especially when embarrassed

brilliant extremely clever and successful

bugle a musical instrument like a small trumpet, used in the army to give signals

charades a game in which some players act out the syllables of a word and the other players try to guess what it is

colonel an army officer of high rank; the head of a regiment

compliment a remark expressing praise or admiration

court *(n)* the official place where the king or queen lives

cunning *(adj & n)* able to get what you want in a clever way, especially by tricking or deceiving somebody

curtsy *(n)* a formal greeting made by a woman by bending her knees with one foot in front of the other

damned *(informal)* a word used to express annoyance, anger, etc.

devoted having great love for somebody and being loyal to them

drawing-room *(old-fashioned)* a room where guests are entertained

faithful loyal; keeping promises to stay with your wife/husband

fellow *(informal)* a way of referring to a man or a boy

121

fireworks paper containers of chemicals that burn or explode, with bright lights and loud noise

fury a feeling of violent anger; *(adj)* **furious**

Gazette the official newspaper of an organization or institution

gloomy dark, miserable; sad and without hope

governess a woman employed by a rich family to live in their home and teach their children

governor a person in charge of a country or region that is politically controlled by another country

guardian someone who is legally responsible for the care of a young person one or both of whose parents are dead

honeymoon a holiday taken by a newly married couple

idiot a foolish person

insurance (life) regular payments to an insurance company so that your family will receive a sum of money when you die

landlord the owner of a house that is rented out to other people

lieutenant an army officer of middle rank (below captain)

lively full of life and energy; full of interest and excitement

major *(n)* an army officer of fairly high rank (below colonel)

miniature a very small detailed painting of a person

mistress the female head of a house, in charge of the servants

neglect *(n & v)* not giving enough care or attention to somebody

noble of a good, often ancient family with a high social position

orphan a child whose parents are dead

Parliament the group of people who are elected to make and change the laws of Great Britain

pension money paid regularly by a rich person to a relative; or by a government to a retired person, a soldier's widow, etc.

regiment a large group of soldiers, commanded by a colonel

reunion when people meet again after being apart for some time

roar *(v & n)* to make a very loud, deep sound; to move very fast, making a lot of noise

roulette a gambling game in which a ball is dropped onto a moving wheel which has holes with numbers on it

settlement (marriage) the financial arrangements agreed for a marriage, including the amount of money to be paid by the bride's family to the husband

shawl a piece of material worn by a woman around her shoulders

sketch-book a book of paper for making simple, quick drawings

slave someone who is so strongly influenced by another person that they will do whatever that person wants

sparkle *(v)* to shine brightly with small flashes of light

style a particular design of clothing; the quality of being elegant and of a high standard; *(adj)* **stylish**

tremendous very great

vanity *(adj* **vain***)* too much pride in your appearance, abilities or achievements; also *(literary)*, the quality of being unimportant, especially compared to other things that are important

weep (past tense **wept**) to cry because you are sad

will *(n)* a legal document which says what is to happen to somebody's money and property after they die

Before Reading

1 Read the story introduction on the first page of the book, and the back cover. One of the girls will wear diamonds, and in the words of a 1940s song, 'Diamonds are a girl's best friend'. Do you think that was also true in Vanity Fair? Discuss these questions.

   1 If Amelia or Becky wears diamonds at an evening party, how will she get them? Will she inherit them, be given them, borrow them, hire them, buy them with her own money, steal them? Might the method be different for each girl?

   2 Of the two girls, which is more likely to wear diamonds? Why?

   3 What does it mean, 'diamonds are a girl's best friend'? Why, in your view, do women want to possess or wear diamonds?

   4 Do you think diamonds are still 'a girl's best friend' today, or do modern girls want other things? If so, what?

2 Here is a list of adjectives that might describe the two heroines. Which adjectives might apply best to Becky, and which to Amelia?

ambitious, amusing, affectionate, brilliant, cunning, devoted, dull, gentle, good, honest, modest, selfish, sensible, strong, sympathetic

3 What are your expectations of a novel like this? Discuss these ideas. Which kind of ending would you prefer?

   1 The 'good' characters will be happy and successful by the end of the story, and the 'bad' will be punished in some way.

   2 The characters will have both 'good' and 'bad' sides to them, and the wicked are just as likely to succeed as the good.

ACTIVITIES

While Reading

Read Chapters 1 to 3. Complete these sentences with names from the story. (Some names will be needed more than once.)

Amelia	George Osborne	Sir Pitt Crawley
Becky	Mr Osborne	Rawdon Crawley
Jos Sedley	William Dobbin	Miss (Matilda) Crawley
Mr Sedley	Miss Briggs	Bute Crawley

1 _____ hoped for a proposal from _____'s brother _____.
2 _____ never spoke of his love for _____, because she was engaged to _____.
3 _____ came to London to look after _____, which upset _____'s devoted companion, _____.
4 _____ had to refuse _____, because she was already married to his son _____.
5 The wealthy _____ planned to divide her money between her nephew _____ and the family of _____.
6 _____ married her beloved _____, even though _____ forbade the marriage when _____ lost all his money.

Before you read on, compare the two newly married couples – Becky and Rawdon, and George and Amelia – and discuss these questions.

7 Which couple is likely to be happier, and why?
8 Which couple is likely to stay together longer, and why?
9 Which couple is more likely to be comfortable financially, and why?

Read Chapters 4 and 5. What do you think might happen in each of these cases?

1 'Becky and Rawdon . . . ran up debts, confident of getting the old lady's money in the end.' *(What if they don't?)*
2 'Hopes on both sides were high – that George's father would forgive him, and that Miss Crawley would forgive Becky and Rawdon.' *(And if they don't, how will each couple react?)*
3 'A tiny flame of jealousy was already burning in Amelia's heart.' *(How will this affect the girls' friendship?)*
4 'There was a note, rolled up like a tiny snake among the flowers.' *(What will happen to this note?)*

Read Chapters 6 to 8, and discuss these questions.

1 How do the two girls compare as mothers?
2 Which girl has the better chance of a successful future?
3 Which girl has the better chance of a happy future?

Before you read on, what do you think lies ahead for the two girls? Give reasons for your choices.

Becky will . . .

4 run away with Lord Steyne.
5 never live with Rawdon again.
6 try to help Rawdon.

Amelia will . . .

7 lose her mind with grief.
8 agree to marry Dobbin.
9 become unexpectedly rich.

Read Chapters 9 and 10. Which of these opinions do you agree with? Give your reasons.

Rawdon . . .

• was right to react as he did, because Becky was guilty.
• was right to be angry, but should have fought Lord Steyne.

- should have kept quiet, as he had been quite happy for Becky to use her charms to their advantage in the past.

Dobbin . . .

- should have stayed in India, because Amelia will never give him the love he deserves.
- should have left Amelia when she said she still thought of George as her husband.
- should stay near Amelia, and try harder to win her love.

Before you read on, what do you think the girls should do now? Give them some advice, using these ideas and your own.

Amelia should . . .

- stop relying on Dobbin to solve her problems.
- marry Dobbin even though she does not love him.
- learn to forget George and love Dobbin.

Becky should . . .

- live a quiet, honest life and find a job as a governess.
- have a brilliant social life in London with Lord Steyne's help.
- try to keep in touch with her son.

Before you read Chapter 11 (*A meeting with an old friend*) and Chapter 12 (*Births, marriages, and deaths*), can you guess what happens?

1 The old friend is _____ and this person meets _____.
2 Births (one): _____
3 Marriages (one): _____
4 Deaths (three): _____

After Reading

1 Here is Rawdon's letter, dictated by Becky, to his brother Pitt (see page 47). Match each of these adjectives with one of the nouns, and complete the letter with the most appropriate pairs of words.

adjectives: *affectionate, charming, excellent, generous, good, great, friendly, happy, loving, warm*

nouns: *attention, brother, eye, fortune, friendship, judgement, memories, nature, pleasure, wife*

My dear Pitt

I am writing to offer sincerest congratulations from Rebecca and myself on your recent _____ _____. There is no doubt that Aunt Matilda showed _____ _____ in leaving her inheritance to you. Of course, in recent years my regimental duties have forced us to live abroad, and as a result we were not able to show Aunt Matilda the _____ _____ that we would have wished. How fortunate that you were able to perform this family duty!

I hear you have returned to Queen's Crawley. (Rebecca and I have such _____ _____ of that house!) As we both know, there has not always been the _____ _____ between us that brothers should enjoy, but I hope that your _____ _____ will allow you to forget our past disagreements. We are both now fathers, and it would give me _____ _____ if our two families could meet as friends. Rebecca and I are most anxious to meet your children and your _____ _____, whom all the world praises, and we beg that you will look with a _____ _____ on our own son, little Rawdy.

Your _____ _____, Rawdon

2 **Perhaps this is what some of the characters in the story were thinking. Which characters are they, who are they thinking about, and what is happening at this point in the story?**

1 'He's a bit upset now, but he'll get over it. And he'll be grateful to me one day. No use getting sentimental about it. There's no point in marrying if there's no money to be had.'

2 'Where on earth is she? It's more than twelve hours now. Why is it taking her so long? She can easily find that much money. Surely she cares enough about me to get me out of here . . .'

3 'I shall like it here – it's certainly better than working for that horrible old man. The old lady isn't too hard to look after, and she's a lot richer! Yes, life will be quite interesting here . . .'

4 'Well, then – it's done. She didn't even look at me as I went out of the door. I hoped she might begin to love me, but it's too soon. It's best I go away. Perhaps after a few years . . .'

5 'Never have I felt so angry in all my life. He is my husband and I have a duty to obey him, but he must see that I cannot be in this house while *she* is here. I must face him at once . . .'

6 'India? Yes, I'd like to go there again. But – I don't know. When I'm with her, I'd do anything for her. But when she goes away, I feel so afraid of – of what she might do.'

7 'It breaks my heart to see him go. I know it will bring him lots of opportunities that he can't have here, and he's so excited about it, but he's my life! Why does nobody understand that?'

8 'Yes, she knows, she knows it's in there! That sparkle in her green eyes says it all! She'll read it when she gets home . . .'

3 Here are some of the more outrageous lies that Becky tells. Rewrite them so that they tell the truth. What do you think would have happened if she had spoken the plain truth?

1 'He's very handsome.' (page 4)
2 'Dearest love, do you suppose that I feel nothing?' (page 46)
3 'I swear that I have done my husband no wrong.' (page 50)
4 'What I should like to do first is to see your dear little children.' (page 62)
5 'Dear, dear Rawdy! I miss him so much.' (page 62)
6 'I have such a headache, and such a heartache!' (page 85)
7 'It was for Rawdon – and you!' (page 90)

4 Here are two entries from different diaries, written one day apart. Choose the best words (one for each gap) to complete the entries. Then say who wrote each entry, and when.

FIRST DIARY

So this is _____ last night in _____ house! I never _____ things to happen _____ quickly. Why didn't _____ Pitt ask me _____? I'm sure the _____ fool won't live _____, and I could _____ been Lady Crawley, _____ and free! It's _____ lucky for me _____ he didn't tell _____ Crawley why I _____ him.

Dear Rawdon! _____ will be fun _____ be together at _____. His greatest talent _____ winning at cards, _____ we'll have a _____ future – if I _____ the decisions and _____ after the money! _____ must stop now _____ write my letter _____ Miss Briggs. I'm _____ I can touch _____ heart with my _____ of true love, _____ then she will _____ Miss Crawley to _____ us, and we _____ be rich.

SECOND DIARY

Oh, what a _____ day! Miss Sharp's _____ gave us all _____ a shock. How _____ that Mrs Bute _____ in time to _____ us! I didn't _____ what to say _____ Miss Crawley. She _____ the news very _____. We had to _____ her to bed _____ call the doctor.

_____ Sir Pitt arrived _____ the house, asking _____ Becky. He was _____ when he heard _____ news, and his _____ was so dreadful _____ I had to _____ the room. I _____ not stop trembling _____ hours afterwards. I _____ tomorrow will be _____ – I don't want _____ more news or _____!

5 **What do you think about the way these people behaved? Was it wicked, foolish, brave, deceitful, bold, practical? Did some of them have excuses for behaving in this way? Discuss your ideas.**

Amelia
• her treatment of Dobbin
• her treatment of her parents after George's death
Becky
• her relationship with Jos Sedley
• her relationship with Lord Steyne
Rawdon
• his card-playing with George and others
• his behaviour after the Lord Steyne affair
Dobbin
• his behaviour towards Amelia
• his relationship with George

6 **Which of the two heroines did you like best? Did they shock, irritate, amuse or fascinate you? Which would you prefer to have as a friend? Why?**

ABOUT THE AUTHOR

William Makepeace Thackeray was born in Calcutta, India, in 1811. He later remembered visions of 'fireworks, and people dancing, and rides on elephants', but his happy early days ended when in 1817 he was sent to England to be educated. He suffered miserably at school, and began studying at Cambridge in 1829, but did not get a degree. Travelling, gambling, drinking, painting, and the company of pretty women were much more to his taste. His search for pleasure took him to London, Weimar in Germany, and Paris, where he is said to have had an affair with a Mademoiselle Pauline, an ex-governess, who may have been the model for Becky Sharp.

The loss of his inheritance, through gambling and several failed investments, forced Thackeray to earn a living, and he turned to journalism, where he had considerable success. In 1836 he married an Irish girl, Isabella Shawe, and the couple returned from Paris to London the following year. They had three daughters, though the second died young, and the marriage was a happy one until Isabella became mentally ill four years later. She never recovered, and Thackeray struggled for some years to cope with this tragedy, seeking a cure for Isabella, writing for newspapers and magazines, including *Punch* and *The Times*, and taking care of his daughters.

Thackeray's early novels, *Catherine* (1839) and *The Luck of Barry Lyndon* (1844), were not successful. *The Book of Snobs* (1846) brought him some popularity, but it was not until *Vanity Fair* appeared that Thackeray began to rival Charles Dickens, who was then at the height of his fame as a novelist. *Vanity Fair* began publication in monthly instalments in January 1847, and at first it did not sell well. Then Mrs Carlyle, a famous literary hostess of the time, after reading the eighth instalment, wrote to her husband that it '. . . beats Dickens out of the world'. Charlotte Brontë praised Thackeray's 'bright wit' and 'attractive humour', and dedicated her novel *Jane Eyre* to him.

The success of the novel was now assured, and Thackeray became a celebrity, which he relished. He also fell in love with Jane Brookfield, the wife of a friend, and his jealousy of her husband was to cause him much anguish. More novels followed, including *Pendennis* (1848–50), and *The History of Henry Esmond* (1852), and Thackeray went on a successful tour of the United States, where he fell briefly in love with a young American woman. 'I can't live without the tenderness of some woman,' he wrote to Jane Brookfield, but increasingly it was his daughters who provided him with companionship and care. He stood unsuccessfully for Parliament at Oxford in 1857, and then returned to writing, with *The Virginians* (1857–59).

In 1860 Thackeray became the first editor of the celebrated *Cornhill Magazine*, but increasing ill health, the legacy of his wild youth, caused him to resign in 1862. He spent his last days in the care of his daughter Annie, and died in London in 1863.

Thackeray has long been acknowledged as one of the greatest English novelists, and *Vanity Fair* is without doubt his greatest work. Early nineteenth-century society is dramatically brought to life, and human virtues and faults and follies are laid bare with great wit and humour. His characters are vividly drawn, and Becky Sharp must be one of the most fascinating heroines of any novel – neither beautiful nor advantaged, but resourceful, quick-thinking, and beguiling in a way that captures the reader just as it does her many admirers.

OXFORD BOOKWORMS LIBRARY

Classics • Crime & Mystery • Factfiles • Fantasy & Horror
Human Interest • Playscripts • Thriller & Adventure
True Stories • World Stories

The OXFORD BOOKWORMS LIBRARY provides enjoyable reading in English, with a wide range of classic and modern fiction, non-fiction, and plays. It includes original and adapted texts in seven carefully graded language stages, which take learners from beginner to advanced level. An overview is given on the next pages.

All Stage 1 titles are available as audio recordings, as well as over eighty other titles from Starter to Stage 6. All Starters and many titles at Stages 1 to 4 are specially recommended for younger learners. Every Bookworm is illustrated, and Starters and Factfiles have full-colour illustrations.

The OXFORD BOOKWORMS LIBRARY also offers extensive support. Each book contains an introduction to the story, notes about the author, a glossary, and activities. Additional resources include tests and worksheets, and answers for these and for the activities in the books. There is advice on running a class library, using audio recordings, and the many ways of using Oxford Bookworms in reading programmes. Resource materials are available on the website <www.oup.com/elt/gradedreaders>.

The *Oxford Bookworms Collection* is a series for advanced learners. It consists of volumes of short stories by well-known authors, both classic and modern. Texts are not abridged or adapted in any way, but carefully selected to be accessible to the advanced student.

You can find details and a full list of titles in the *Oxford Bookworms Library Catalogue* and *Oxford English Language Teaching Catalogues*, and on the website <www.oup.com/elt/gradedreaders>.

THE OXFORD BOOKWORMS LIBRARY
GRADING AND SAMPLE EXTRACTS

STARTER • 250 HEADWORDS

present simple – present continuous – imperative –
can/cannot, must – *going to* (future) – simple gerunds …

Her phone is ringing – but where is it?

Sally gets out of bed and looks in her bag. No phone. She looks under the bed. No phone. Then she looks behind the door. There is her phone. Sally picks up her phone and answers it. *Sally's Phone*

STAGE I • 400 HEADWORDS

… past simple – coordination with *and, but, or* –
subordination with *before, after, when, because, so* …

I knew him in Persia. He was a famous builder and I worked with him there. For a time I was his friend, but not for long. When he came to Paris, I came after him – I wanted to watch him. He was a very clever, very dangerous man. *The Phantom of the Opera*

STAGE 2 • 700 HEADWORDS

… present perfect – *will* (future) – *(don't) have to, must not, could* –
comparison of adjectives – simple *if* clauses – past continuous –
tag questions – *ask/tell* + infinitive …

While I was writing these words in my diary, I decided what to do. I must try to escape. I shall try to get down the wall outside. The window is high above the ground, but I have to try. I shall take some of the gold with me – if I escape, perhaps it will be helpful later. *Dracula*

STAGE 3 • 1000 HEADWORDS

... should, may – present perfect continuous – *used to* – past perfect –
causative – relative clauses – indirect statements ...

Of course, it was most important that no one should see
Colin, Mary, or Dickon entering the secret garden. So Colin
gave orders to the gardeners that they must all keep away
from that part of the garden in future. ***The Secret Garden***

STAGE 4 • 1400 HEADWORDS

... past perfect continuous – passive (simple forms) –
would conditional clauses – indirect questions –
relatives with *where/when* – gerunds after prepositions/phrases ...

I was glad. Now Hyde could not show his face to the world
again. If he did, every honest man in London would be proud
to report him to the police. ***Dr Jekyll and Mr Hyde***

STAGE 5 • 1800 HEADWORDS

... future continuous – future perfect –
passive (modals, continuous forms) –
would have conditional clauses – modals + perfect infinitive ...

If he had spoken Estella's name, I would have hit him. I was so
angry with him, and so depressed about my future, that I could
not eat the breakfast. Instead I went straight to the old house.
Great Expectations

STAGE 6 • 2500 HEADWORDS

... passive (infinitives, gerunds) – advanced modal meanings –
clauses of concession, condition

When I stepped up to the piano, I was confident. It was as if I
knew that the prodigy side of me really did exist. And when I
started to play, I was so caught up in how lovely I looked that
I didn't worry how I would sound. ***The Joy Luck Club***